COYOTES & CANARIES

Other books by Larry K. Brown

The Hog Ranches of Wyoming
Petticoat Prisoners of the Wyoming Frontier Prison
You Are Respectfully Invited to Attend My Execution
Petticoat Prisoners of Old Wyoming

COYOTES & CANARIES

Characters Who Made the West Wild
...and Wonderful!

Larry K. Brown

with a foreword by
former Wyoming Governor Mike Sullivan

High Plains Press

Library of Congress Cataloging-in-Publication Data

Brown, Larry K.
  Coyotes and canaries : characters who made the West wild and
wonderful! / Larry K. Brown ; with a foreword by former Wyoming
governor Mike Sullivan.
        p. cm.
Includes bibliographical references and index.
    ISBN 0-931271-69-X (limited ed. : alk. paper) --
    ISBN 0-931271-70-3 (trade pbk. : alk. paper)
1. Wyoming--Biography. 2. Wyoming--History--Anecdotes.
3. Pioneers--Wyoming--Biography. 4. Politicians--Wyoming--
Biography. 5. Indians of North America--Wyoming--Biography.
I. Title.
F760 .B76 2002
978.7'009'9--dc21
                                                    2002009832

For a catalogue or information contact:
High Plains Press
P.O. Box 123, Glendo, Wyoming 82213
Ph. 1-800-552-7819
www.highplainspress.com

For the Browns

—Jeremiah, Mentor, Ulysses, and Mentor II—

whose love of language and telling of tales

guide my work and add joy to my life.

❧ CONTENTS ❧

*A*s a young boy, some of my most cherished hours were spent in my grandparents' basement in Laramie, Wyoming. It was filled wall to wall with the memories of more than fifty years—discarded clothes, books, medals, guns, papers, musical instruments, and wonderful memorabilia. One could spend a whole day exploring, imagining and dreaming about the stories these items represented. In part, what Larry Brown has done with *Coyotes and Canaries* is the same, though he has rummaged through a much larger basement, the Wyoming State Museum, and covered a much longer period in history. Utilizing his considerable talents and experience as an author/journalist/researcher, he has put down on paper marvelous stories laced with both imagination and reality. These stories bring to life the history, times, and events associated with objects found in the Museum as well as the people—some larger than life—and places connected to those artifacts.

I have long admired Larry for his talent, enthusiasm, and energy. Over the years, his regular articles in the *Casper Star-Tribune* have entertained Wyoming readers while deepening their interest in history and adding fresh knowledge to it. Little did I appreciate, however, when asked to contribute a foreword to *Coyotes and Canaries*, how much pleasure I would experience in reading the compiled articles, some for the first time. Nor did I anticipate what vivid mental images Larry would generate—images of colorful characters and unique and exciting times in the history of the West, the Wyoming Territory, and the State of Wyoming. I envy both Larry's willingness to undertake this effort, and the curiosity which drives him to venture far from the "basement" and extend his research and personal interviews to other locations, adding color and character—and there is a wealth of both—to his stories.

Brown introduces us to fascinating personalities, beginning and ending with two of Wyoming's colorful women (both prostitutes). He also offers historical context; for example, I had not appreciated that the Mormons, led by Brigham Young, crossed Wyoming on their way to Utah in 1847, nearly thirty years before Crazy Horse and Custer held their famous get-together on the Little Big Horn. This book is a salute to those whose contributions have helped make Wyoming the wonderful and wild place it was and is. Whether showing us the steely perseverance and toughness of Jackson Sundown or Chief Washakie, the hardened immorality of Tom Horn or Big Nose George Parrott, the unique artistic and creative talents of photographer Joseph Stimson and furniture maker Thomas Molesworth, the vision of Grace Raymond Hebard and Esther Hobart Morris, or the unfortunate treatment and fate of the Chinese miners, *Coyotes and Canaries* provides a marvelous trip into Wyoming's past.

I won't even venture into Larry's fanciful interview with my own Stetson, which now rests comfortably in the State Museum, except to say that hat did accompany me on an eight-year adventure and a rare privilege afforded me by the people of Wyoming (see chapter 42: "A Chat with a Hat"). The memory of those times will always be my most cherished as an adult, for, while now history to some and hopefully affording some basement memories for my grandchildren, it was a very real, fulfilling, and challenging time for me and my wife, Jane. For bringing other chapters of Wyoming's colorful past to life, we are indebted to the time and talent of Larry K. Brown and those who helped him along the extraordinary—and no doubt from time to time bumpy—trails he pursued to bring us *Coyotes and Canaries*. This is a book that will provide pleasure, adventure, and an expanded knowledge of a wonderful state and its history.

MIKE SULLIVAN
GOVERNOR OF WYOMING
1987–1995

The idea for this book originated early in 1996 when Linda Fabian, then manager of the Public Information Office for Wyoming's Department of Commerce, asked me if I would consider continuing a series of articles for the *Casper Star-Tribune* featuring Wyoming State Museum relics and rarities. Titled "Wyoming Artifacts," the series had been written by the museum's staff. I served as a volunteer at that time in Linda's office. Delighted with the subject matter, as well as the opportunity to learn about a wide variety of fascinating objects—some seldom seen or touched—I accepted her offer and immediately began researching and writing the articles.

Little did I know, nor could I have anticipated, that the venture would let me delve into the lives of some of the most intriguing historical figures in Wyoming—indeed in all the West. Such characters include Dr. Lillian Heath, who "gave" me the title for this book. While researching her career as Wyoming's first woman physician, I found in her papers a sheet headed "Favorite Things." Dr. Heath had listed her best-loved authors, painters, playwright, sculptors, and so on. Opposite "Musicians," she had written "coyotes and canaries." Clearly, I believe, she felt a heartfelt link with the beast's soulful howl at day's end, even as she loved the bird's cheerful chirp and trill. I immediately was struck not only by the wonderful imagery and alliteration, but it occurred to me that her coyotes and canaries might serve as metaphors for many of the Old West folk who I find most interesting. Take the wild and wily coyote, whose stealth and taste for barnyard fowl and small pets make him a feared and despised predator. So, too, is the outlaw, knave, and seemingly ever-present rogue who tend to soil our lives. And then there is that small, fine-feathered yellow bird, with its bright song that makes our ears dance and our hearts sing. Ah yes! It represents the caregivers, soul savers, and those who give love. The canary also brings to mind the artists, the innovators, the pathfinders, as well as those who create things which please us and enrich our lives.

But the more I learned about my each of my protagonists, the more I understood that none was exclusively a coyote or a canary. Each, in fact, had elements of both…the yin and the yang…the bad and the beautiful. And those characteristics not only endeared them to me, but inspired me to capture and record their stories for future generations.

For example, I learned the tales of **Lou Polk** and **Dell Burke** and how those soiled doves not only survived but prospered by trading their bodies for money…**"Big Nose" George Parrott**, who sold his soul by theft and the stolen lives of others… **"Ella" Watson** and **Jim Averell** who, due to the greed of others, danced to death at the ends of ropes…some thirty **Chinese coal miners**, who lost their lives to racist, covetous competitors…black state legislator **William Jefferson Hardin**, who tasted the fruits of fame and fortune, then lost all with a self-inflicted gunshot. There are other notables, too: writer **Owen Wister**…suffragette and historian **Grace Raymond Hebard** …artist **Juan Menchaca**…cattle baron **Alexander Hamilton Swan** …religious leader **Brigham Young**…Justice of the Peace **Esther Hobart Morris**…Shoshone **Chief Washakie**…world champion saddle bronc rider **Jackson Sundown**…Wild West hero and international showman **William Frederick "Buffalo Bill" Cody**…**Heart Mountain Japanese internees** and many more.

And if I have done them justice by telling their tales well, my friends listed here must share in that success. At the top of that list, of course, are Linda Fabian, Cathy Lujan, and Melinda Brazzale, all of whom served with the Wyoming Department of Commerce's now defunct Public Information Office. Without their daily encouragement and unfailing support, most of these stories would never have been written.

The *Casper Star-Tribune's* former "Focus" section chief, K.C. Compton, and her associate, Judy Hamilton, too, have my deep appreciation for their professional editorial guidance and assistance.

My thanks go also to the Wyoming State Museum's excellent staff, most specifically Jennifer Alexander and Dominique Schultes.

Those highly skilled individuals suggested many of the subjects for my articles and most generously shared their expertise, knowledge, and records to ensure each of my stories is based on the most accurate curatorial information available.

The Wyoming State Archives staff—particularly Cindy Brown and Ann Nelson, as well as former senior historians Jean Brainerd and LaVaugh Bresnahan—also provided "above and beyond" service not only by patiently and cheerfully answering my nearly endless questions, but by generously offering their time and talents to satisfy my every request for supporting historical data. And without the superior help of former photographic curator Craig Pindell and his successor, Carol Barber, as well as Richard Collier, the Wyoming State Historical Preservation Office's photographer, these stories would not be nearly so well illustrated.

And of course, without my publisher Nancy Curtis's trust, confidence, and support, there would be no book.

Lastly, as in all past personal and professional endeavors, I am indebted to Florence—my wife, friend, mate, and life's compass —who touched each of the stories with her innate sense of propriety, historical perspective, and fine Irish humor.

LARRY K. BROWN

CHEYENNE, WYOMING

*B*ecause Wyoming's history and some of its most interesting characters are the focus of this book, I conducted most of my research at the Wyoming State Archives and the Wyoming State Museum, both of which are located in the Barrett Building at 2301 Central Avenue in Cheyenne, Wyoming.

The Wyoming State Archives offers perhaps the most complete and diversified collection of officially maintained public state records in Wyoming, many of which date back to the origin of the territorial government. These include not only the documents and correspondence of elected officials and their respective offices, but also those of many religious and fraternal organizations as well as U.S. government military records from the various frontier Army posts that made the settlement of Wyoming possible. Available, too, are collections of personal correspondence, diaries, and memoirs from some the state's most prominent pioneers and many subsequent citizens, as well as records of births, marriages, deaths, divorces, and burials.

The facility's wealth of research aids eased my study considerably. These include indexes on a wide variety of subjects, card catalogs, microfilms (cited as "MA" in this book), manuscripts ("MS" and "MSS"), historic corporate business papers, and files of most of the newspapers ever published in Wyoming.

Also found there is a superlative collection of historic photographs, some of which illustrate this book. Handwritten on the backs of many of those prints are notes and descriptions that contain information about the past that may not be found anywhere else.

The Wyoming State Museum, too, is a trove of treasures. There I found many items that my subjects made or used, and also documentation—the "who, what, when, where, and why"—describing how these artifacts reflected on their lives and Wyoming's history.

Dedicated researchers will also value the accession files: the correspondence and other documents that trace the history of each relic. They detail each item's transfer of ownership from its donor to the repository that is Wyoming's largest for such artifacts, and widely considered its most prestigious. They also describe each artifact, its composition, its condition, its purpose, and most particularly its care and maintenance by museum curators.

And I would be remiss if I did not mention that a helpful staff is available at each of those facilities to answer questions and guide visitors in their respective searches through history.

At the end of each chapter, in the "Sources Cited" section, I have listed the primary and secondary materials used, and interviews I conducted, in researching these subjects. I have cited only those sources that I believe to be the most important of the many I consulted.

Readers may note that some passages quoted in this book contain misspellings, grammatical errors, or other inconsistencies. These have been retained for the sake of authenticity, and for the extra flavor they often convey.

L.K.B.

CHAPTER 1

Louella Polk

A NOSE FOR TROUBLE

THOSE FEW WHO chanced to see the woman veiled in black knew better than to stare. For as she trod the hot, clay streets of Casper, Wyoming that late summer of 1890, Mrs. Louella Polk made clear her foul mood. She had lost her love, her business, and her nose.

Exactly when Lou, as most knew her, had arrived in Casper is not clear. Her name first appeared in the city's records on September 4, 1889, when authorities convicted her as one of fifteen "inmates of houses of ill fame" and she paid a three-dollar fine plus two dollars in costs.

Her earliest history is equally vague. She came into this world in Missouri sometime before May 11, 1867, as a child of Armillia Woolsey, whose maiden name remains unknown. About her father we know only his last name, Woolsey. Lou and her mother next surfaced in 1880 at Cheyenne, Wyoming, where their names appear in the territorial census as the daughter and wife, respectively, of Charles W. Harvicker, a thirty-seven-year-old painter.

Although available records show no divorce, Lou's parents had separated by July 10, 1883. Armillia then leased a "sixty feet long by twenty four feet, one story frame building situated close to Lake Sloan," at that time a mile or so north of Cheyenne. She apparently planned to operate the place as a roadhouse, or at least to take in boarders. Almost immediately, however, she fell behind in her payments, so on May 10 of the following year owner Mathew Sloan sued her for his rent.

Whether to circumvent the lawsuit or simply to add much-needed income to their purses, Armillia, Louella, and the recently widowed Mrs. Dora Mills, who shared their home, immediately decided to marry their local boyfriends. So suddenly did they make their decisions

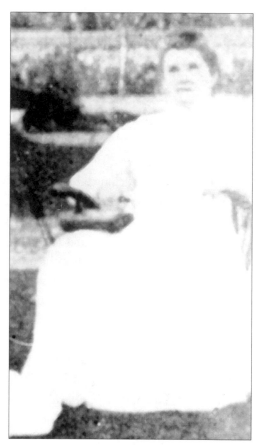

Armillia Woolsey Robertson, a prominent member of the Natrona County Pioneer Society, set tongues wagging in her younger years when she staged a triple wedding on the shores of Sloan's Lake north of Cheyenne. Armillia summoned a justice of the peace in the wee morning hours to the house she shared with her daughter, Lou, and a friend, Dora Mills. For a free buggy ride and a liberal fee, the sleepy official wed the three ladies to local boyfriends. Regrettably, there is no known photo of Lou. (Wyoming State Archives)

to wed that they roused Laramie County's assistant county clerk from his sleep the very next night—Saturday, May 11—and asked him to procure the proper marriage documents at the courthouse.

Soon thereafter, J.W. Fisher, the local justice of the peace, also got a request from the ladies. He, too, agreed to do his duty, but only if they furnished "a good, easy carriage" to take him to their lakeside home. After settling those arrangements, Judge Fisher rode out to the women's place where, for a fee, he united the three couples before a small group of friends at about one o'clock in the morning.

What apparently began with such hope ended several years later when Armillia and Lou separated from their spouses. Although history does not record why the couples split, Lou remarried on July 21, 1886, at Fort Laramie. This time she wed twenty-seven-year-old

William Estes Polk, who had managed northern Wyoming's famed Keeline Cattle Company. That union also soon failed, so Lou and her mother moved northwest to Douglas. There Polk's brother had a gambling house and saloon. Chronology and circumstances suggest that during this period Lou, a "rather tall, magnetic type of fine figure, quite good looking," discovered the bright lights, the fast life, and a talent for what became her profession.

Not long after, Lou and the infamous "Dogae" Lee May (sometimes spelled Mai) became partners in Casper's Dance House until a squabble sent Lou back to her mother in Douglas. Burdened with mounting debts, however, Dogae coaxed Lou to return to Casper in the spring of 1890 to help sell their dance hall.

Casper had been incorporated only about two years earlier. Its businesses consisted mostly of "sporting houses": gambling joints, saloons, and brothels, as well as Casper's one and only "dance house," Lou's joint east and across the alley from Center Street. There two drinks—one for the customer and one for a soiled dove—also entitled the couple to one dance. Thence the Dance House derived its name. But as any red-blooded fellow knows, one twirl to a tune is never enough. And so those with more money than good sense might linger in the dance hall where local toughs regularly rousted and robbed them before they kicked them into the street.

The city fathers kept the sporting establishments separated from residential neighborhoods with an early form of zoning that served several purposes. For one thing, limiting such establishments to a prescribed area made them easier to police. Authorities restricted saloons to within what is now the 200 block of Center Street, while they made sure most of the "cribs," the shacks where girls entertained their customers, remained west and across the alley at the rear of the saloons facing David Street.

Such zoning served at least two other practical ends. First, it restricted the din that might continue from night to morn, as each joint had its own "piano thumper." Second, the town's unreliable water pump was placed at the hub of such all-night activities, accessible to those sober enough to man it in case of fire.

CENTER STREET. CASPER. WYO. 1890.

Casper city fathers in 1890 separated the sporting houses from residential areas to help policing. Saloons stood within what is now the 200 block of Center Street, while most "cribs," where the good-time girls entertained, were across the alley and to the rear of the bars. (Wyoming State Archives)

Fourteen-year-old sheepherder John "Charlie" Rate first noted the trouble between Lou and her erstwhile paramour. A couple of days after Lou had returned to Casper, Charlie drove a supply wagon down Casper Creek, about two miles from town. Hearing a scream, he turned to see a woman on horseback ride towards him, her hair fluttering in a wide wake of dust as she frantically lashed her steed. A slim, beady-eyed horseman pursued her, trying to load his revolver.

Just before the gunman caught her near the herder's wagon, she cried, "I'm Lou and he's Dogae." When the gunman ordered her to "move on," she leaped to the ground instead. With that, he pulled down on her with his six-shooter and warned her to remount or die. As she climbed back astride her horse, Dogae snatched the reins from her hands and barked, "Come on, you ———; we're going to the British Possessions."

Before they left, the brute warned young Charlie that if he breathed a word of what he had seen, he would come back and cut out his heart. In the midst of that confusion, Lou dropped her quirt into the wagon as a mute appeal for help. Then she and her captor crossed the bridge over the Platte River and disappeared into the surrounding sandhills. Charlie so feared Dogae, who some claimed had fled Texas after being charged with murder, that the boy kept silent.

Later that day, when a workman at Shorty Castle's livery barn recognized the riding whip, Charlie still felt so intimidated by Dogae that he lied and said he found it in the road. Only when night passed and the couple failed to return did the boy tell authorities of his fears for Lou's safety. Sheriff William W. Jaycox quickly gathered a posse and started in pursuit, but the trail had already been obliterated by rain.

Later, Lou recalled the terror of her experience to a *Wyoming Derrick* reporter. Her words appeared in the first edition of that newspaper on May 21, 1890.

> *We started out, I supposed, for a pleasure ride, but from the time we were seen by the sheepherder… I was an unwilling prisoner. Dogae forced me to accompany him by means of all kinds of horrible threats and a six-shooter. Sometimes he said he would kill me, and again that he was going to take me to Kansas. We rode without food for two days, when Dogae killed a rabbit, and we ate part of it raw in a cabin near Fetterman. Then we went without a morsel of food for four whole days, traveling nights and hiding in the bushes along the streams during the day… [Several days later] we were hid in a gulch when I happened to raise my head and saw Sheriff Jaycox passing a few hundred yards away. Dogae saw him at the same time, and pulling me to the ground placed his six-shooter to my ear and said if I moved he would blow my brains out.*

Unaware that the fugitives hid nearby, the posse continued on to Tom Hood's sheep camp near Fish Creek, where the sheriff asked the herders to be on the lookout for the missing couple. If they found the pair, they should disarm Dogae and hold him until the law could be called.

Dogae and Lou, haggard and hungry, arrived at the sheep camp about three hours later, but instead of following the sheriff's orders, two herders there only warned the visitors to give up and return to Casper.

At this livery barn a workman found Lou Polk's riding crop in sheepherder Charlie Rate's supply wagon. Rate lied that he found it in the road, fearing that if he told the truth, Lou's lover would return to cut out his heart. (Frances Seely Webb Collection, Casper College)

Dogae, feigning agreement, turned over their horses to the men and said he would ask their foreman for train passage back to Casper. But as soon as the boys broke camp, Dogae took Lou to the sheep foreman's cabin, where he chased off the foreman and forced Lou inside.

What happened next proved so vicious...so macabre, that decency demands the details be spared. What can be told is that after Dogae threw Lou to the floor, he jumped astride her struggling body and swore that "If I can't have you, I'll make you so damned ugly that nobody else will want you." Then, with a keen knife, he slashed off her nose and threw the bloody part across the room. Satisfied that she "was ugly enough," he stormed out of the cabin with the foreman's Winchester rifle, then stole the man's best horse and a saddle and rode away.

Quickly the foreman returned to a most terrible scene: there stood Lou holding her severed nose in a dampened handkerchief. The foreman harnessed a team, loaded Lou into his wagon, and rushed east to Wendover, a nearby railroad town, where steady hands tried to reattach her nose with a bandage of "court plaster."

When that failed, mail carrier T.J. Montgomery drove Lou in his dray some forty-two miles northwest along the North Platte River to Douglas so that Dr. Amos Barber could treat her. Unfortunately the physician failed, too, despite his best efforts.

In the meantime, authorities filed "horse stealing" charges against Dogae and soon a posse of six, spurred by a $200 reward for his capture, rode in pursuit. While lawmen searched unsuccessfully for the felon, court-ordered civil judgments obligated Lou and Dogae to pay off their creditors. But Dogae was never brought to justice.

❧

During Lou's physical and financial recovery, she wore a false nose of wood or wax that she hooked over her ears like spectacles when she left home. With the psychological aid of that device, which she concealed with a heavy black veil even on the warmest days, Lou took control of the Dance House. She also continued to ply her trade and pay her monthly fines as an "ill-famed" denizen.

Perhaps because of her precarious health, she soon sold an interest in her business to John Lawrence of Douglas. Whatever the reason, Wilson S. Kimball, editor of the *Wyoming Derrick*, applauded her decision. "Considering that such institutions are a necessity in this western country," he wrote, "the house could not be in better hands. John will keep an orderly place." Lawrence had co-owned an infamous "hog ranch"—a rural phenomenon of the 1800s that combined the entertaining elements of a saloon, gambling hall, and brothel—several years earlier at the abandoned Fort Fetterman.

Despite his experience in the "water trade," even Lawrence could not control the henna-haired hellion who became increasingly irascible following her last ordeal with Dogae. On August 9 authorities arrested her for "keeping a disorderly house." She pled innocent, but witnesses convinced Justice of the Peace R.H. Weber that the accusations were "well founded." Apparently the judge agreed because he found Lou guilty and fined her a total of $10.30.

John Conway, a dance-hall bouncer, earned the distinction of being Casper's first convicted murderer when he shot and killed A.J. "Red Jack" Tidwell in a drunken brawl. (Wyoming State Archives)

Lou's travails with the law climaxed on Saturday night, September 20, 1890. At about ten o'clock, James "Jimmy" Hines and Will Demarest, a couple of local cowboys, entered the Dance House and began to devil H.J. "Sonny" Summers, Jr., a violinist playing there. Lou's bartender-bouncer, John "Jack" C. Conway, immediately stepped in and demanded that the boys leave the Summers lad alone.

A short time later, the drunken Hines and A.J. "Red Jack" Tidwell, a cowpoke from the FL Ranch, returned and again began to rough up the fiddle player. This time when Conway tried to intercede, Tidwell punched him in the face. The bartender returned the favor. Then, after pushing the cowpoke back against a monte table near the south door, Conway ordered him to leave ... *pronto!*

When Tidwell rushed back brandishing a large knife, Conway bolted behind the bar and grabbed a .38-caliber Colt revolver. "I'll fix him," he cried, with weapon in hand. The sight of Conway angrily waving the pistol scattered the three dozen unarmed customers and the girls who worked there. The crowd fled out the north exit and into the streets. Worse, Sonny, the abused fiddler, raced from the door only to gouge out his left eye on a dead fir tree limb propped there, a remnant of the past July Fourth decorations.

Inside the hall, Tidwell must have had second thoughts about tangling with Lou's bouncer. Declaring "I'm going," he, too, raced toward the door as Conway chased his heels. But once outside, Tidwell spun and grabbed Conway. In the ensuing scuffle, Conway allegedly bashed the cowboy's head with his pistol. As Tidwell fell, or as he lay dazed on the ground (according to some reports), Conway shot him in the left side. The bullet severed Tidwell's femoral artery and burst out of his skin just above his right hip.

As Tidwell lay bleeding to death, Laura Olsen, one of Lou's working girls, ran into the nearby Patton & Nickelson Saloon, where Constable Hugh L. "Colorado" Patton, having heard the shot, went behind the bar to get his own gun. "Oh, come quick!" cried the young woman. "They are fighting and shooting over at the Dance Hall."

Patton ran to the scene, where Conway greeted him. "Well, I guess I am your prisoner. This is the gun that did the business." When the lawman asked him what he had done, Conway responded, "I knocked a lame fellow down and shot at him. I expect I killed him."

Tidwell's friends became so incensed that only the wile of Sheriff Jaycox saved Conway from a lynching. How? Well, he had the cowboy's funeral delayed until the next night, so that he could move the bartender from the jail into a nearby railway car while local clergy conducted the services. The next through train then took Conway out of town to safety.

Neither Jaycox nor the city marshal, however, could prevent an attempt by the dead cowboy's friends to torch the Dance House four

Hugh "Colorado" Patton, acting constable on the evening of September 20, 1890, was called to Lou Polk's notorious Dance House, where the first of Casper's many murders took place. Patton subsequently served two terms as Natrona County sheriff and, still later, as a Wyoming state legislator. (Natrona County Sheriff's Department)

nights later. Arsonists poured kerosene on the front door and floor and lit it with a match. Luckily, one of the men inside discovered the blaze and extinguished it before it could do major damage.

The law subsequently brought Conway to court, where it tried and convicted the former railroad brakeman from Colorado for murder before sending him off to the Wyoming State Penitentiary at Laramie. But some blamed Lou for Casper's first homicide. *Wyoming Derrick* editor Kimball wrote in his May 21, 1890, issue:

> *Ever since her escapade last spring, wherein Lou Polk was forcibly abducted by "Dogae," a reckless adventurer with whom*

Sheriff William W. Jaycox, fearing for Lou Polk's safety, raised a posse of volunteers to search the surrounding countryside for the missing dance-hall queen. Although Lou later was found alive at a sheep camp, her nose and her vicious partner "Dogae" Lee were missing. (Sheriff Louis Cooper Collection, Casper College)

she had been cohabiting and who had become jealous of her, and who cut off her nose upon being compelled to abandon her owing to the close pursuit of officers, she has imagined herself a heroine, or "bad man" as it were. She assumed entire control of the dance house which she and "Dogae" had formerly owned in partnership, and set herself up as "Queen of the Demi-monde." Her word was law in the establishment, and she delighted to show her authority. She breeds more discontent and trouble than any other dozen characters in the town, and when she finally obtained the service of John Conaway [sic], it is said she boasted that she "had a man-killer, and would like to see the person, who dared to kick up a row in her house." On the afternoon of the killing she purchased the weapon with which the murder was committed, and it is probable that Conaway had been encouraged to use it in case [a] row should occur. The Derrick does not in the least object to bawdy houses, nor even to dance houses, or to the class of people who inhabit the same, realizing as we do that they are in a measure a necessity in this Western country (to insure the safety of respectable women), but Mrs. Lulu Polk is a nuisance that should be abated. Even the sporting element must agree with us in this opinion, for a few more "breaks" like she has made might result in all peoples of that class being excluded from town a state of affairs that we should dislike to see.

Kimball's inked diatribe so incensed Lou and her mother that they went to the *Derrick* office and threatened to horsewhip him. But after her creditors again successfully sued her, and she faced the real threat of being tarred, feathered, and run out of town on a rail, Lou left Casper.

Little is known about her next few years, but old-timers said she retreated west and settled in Fallon, Nevada.

In the meantime Lou's mother, Armillia, married Donald "Dan" A. Robertson, a successful Canadian saloonkeeper in Douglas. The following year the couple moved to Casper, where Robertson prospered as a bar owner. In fact, his popularity led to his election as Natrona County's representative in the 1903 State Legislature. And thanks in part to his growing prominence as well as to her own absence from the scene, Lou's notoriety gradually subsided. Even so, she did not reappear in Casper until June 1907 when she became terminally ill with tuberculosis and her mother brought her back to Wyoming. Lou died in her mother's house two months later on Friday, August 17, at the age of forty. Prior to the three o'clock funeral services on Sunday when they bid her farewell at her mother's home, Lou's family placed her in a "beautiful casket...covered with flowers sent by friends and relatives."

Donald "Dan" A. Robertson, a Canadian, met and married Lou Polk's mother in Douglas, Wyoming. After later moving to Casper, the prosperous saloonkeeper helped establish fraternal lodges there for the Masons and the Elks before becoming Natrona County's first state legislator. (Wyoming State Archives)

In deference to the respected and well-liked Robertsons, Casper old-timers refrained from discussing Lou's past and tenaciously refused to reveal to the next generation the name under which Lou had been interred. Nor would they tell exactly where her family had buried her—fearing, they said, that vandals might desecrate her headstone. But those interested in such macabre history will find the truth in the Robertsons' family plot at Casper's Highland Cemetery. There, beneath a headstone labeled Mrs. Lulu Cocoran, lie the mortal remains of Lou Polk.

Louella Polk rests in the family plot with her mother and stepfather, having lost her virtue, her lover, her business, and her nose to the sins of a misspent life. (Author's collection)

❧ SOURCES CITED ❧ Several primary source materials and official records were especially valuable in authenticating Lou Polk's early life, as well as her later brushes with the law. These include the Laramie County Marriage Records, May 10–11, 1884, Vol. 2, and the Justice of the Peace and Police Justice Docket of R.H. Wilber, Natrona County, Casper, Wyoming Territory, which can be found at the Wyoming State Archives in Cheyenne. The Converse County Marriage Records (Book 23) at the courthouse in Douglas also shed light on Lou's marital experiences. As to the murder of A.J. "Red Jack" Tidwell, much of the incriminating evidence is recorded in *State of Wyoming v. John C. Conway*, Judicial District Court Criminal Court Case #4, on file at the Natrona County District Court Clerk's Office in Casper. The 1880 Wyoming Territorial Census at the Wyoming State Archives also helped verify facts about the lives of Lou and her relatives.

One must turn to the Sexton's Records (Burials 1893–1914, Vols. 1 and 2, Microfilm #H-184) at the State Archives to find details about Lou's burial site.

But the most colorful details about Lou and her terrifying relationship with "Dogae" Lee were documented by one who probably knew the pair as well as any: Wilson S. Kimball. As editor of the *Wyoming Derrick* at the time the couple's split cost Lou her nose, Kimball reported those gory details in his page-one story, "A Devil's Deed," in the first issue (May 21, 1890) of his publication. Subsequent editions (especially June 19, July 10, and September 25, 1890), continued to track her troubles. More accounts of Lou and those who played key roles in her life also appeared in other local newspapers, such as the *Cheyenne Democratic Leader* (May 13, 1884) and the *Cheyenne Daily Sun* (May 13, 1884); *Casper Weekly Mail* (March 1, 1889), *Natrona County Tribune*, and a contemporary feature in the *Casper Star-Tribune* (July 17, 1980).

The works of several Natrona County historians helped flesh out many of the highs and lows in her troubled life. These include Alfred James Mokler's *History of Natrona County, Wyoming 1888–1922* (Chicago: R.R. Donnelley & Sons Company, 1923), Edness Kimball Wilkins's *Casper Chronicles* (Casper, WY: Casper Zonta Club, 1964), and Mary Helen Hendry's *Petticoats & Pistols* (Casper, WY: Mountain State Lithographing, 1992). These books also document life in Casper's earliest days. So does Phil McAuley's article "Ill Wind Blew No Good for Noseless Lady" that appeared in the July 17, 1980 *Casper Star-Tribune* under the columnist's "McAuley's Wyoming" banner.

And lastly, Elnora L. Frye's *Atlas of Wyoming Outlaws at the Territorial Penitentiary* (Laramie, WY: Jelm Mountain Publications, 1990) summarizes John C. Conway's history and prison records.

This chapter first appeared, in a slightly different form, in *Old West* magazine (Summer 1996).

CHAPTER 2

CHARLES M. ADAMS

THE MASKED RIDER OF LARAMIE PEAK

At this point they caught sight of 30 to 40 windmills which were standing on the plain there, and no sooner had Don Quixote laid eyes upon them than he turned to his squire and said, "... You see there before you, friend Sancho Panza, some 30 or more lawless giants with whom I mean to do battle. I shall deprive them of their lives ... for this is warfare, and it is a great service to God to remove so accursed a breed from the face of the earth.

—Don Quixote, Cervantes

ASTRIDE A snow-white horse and wearing a black mask that covered all but his eyes, the Masked Rider was first seen one warm summer night in 1930 near Laramie Peak in eastern Wyoming. His roughly scrawled handwritten signs, however, had preceded him, warning those he opposed to leave the country or suffer the consequences.

It was about 10:45 on the night of June 9 that year when rancher William Atkinson was called to the outer entry of his kitchen. As he half-opened the door, a masked man—with his hat tied down over his face—pulled his pistol. Instinctively, Atkinson slammed the latch shut and jumped aside as a slug ripped through the wood, missing him by inches. Mounting a horse that was draped with a light gray blanket, the assailant sped off into the night. A white cardboard sign found later on Atkinson's step threatened: "This is the last warning. leave or you will be killed. the Masked Rider."

... he gave spurs to his steed Rocinante, without paying any heed to Sancho's warning that these were truly windmills and not giants that he was riding forth to attack.

Poor Charlie Adams! His vivid imagination and love of western dime novels led him into a misadventure that blazed across the front pages of newspapers throughout the nation in 1930. (Wheatland Times, Wheatland, Wyoming, August 14, 1930)

Although the authorities were called immediately, the case was hard to solve. Rumors were rife. Confusion reigned. Each new report of a sighting fueled a firestorm of media coverage, even making national headlines that summer. First the Rider was a moonshiner trying to protect his still. Next he was a rustler. Some thought he meant to scare off a rival lover. He was dead. He was captured. His pursuers even suggested that he reversed the rear shoes on his horse to confuse those who tried to follow.

Hand-penciled signs and typed notes continued to chase and chastise those whom the phantom perceived as evildoers. No one seemed to attract the Rider's wrath more than twenty-year-old

Charles M. Adams. The slender youth with blue eyes and a reddish complexion worked for rancher Charles Wagner. Adams was relaxing in his bunkhouse on the night of July 18 when a bullet tore through his left shoulder. It barely missed his heart. Sid Sturgeon, who was visiting the ranch, heard the shot and raced to the scene where he found the young man wounded. The cowboy, weak from loss of blood, was rushed to the hospital in nearby Wheatland where he slowly recovered.

The young range rider claimed it was the third attempt on his life. Six months earlier, he said, someone had fired a bullet from ambush that ripped a hole in the leg of his pants. Then in early July, another shot from a brush draw had creased the pommel of his saddle. Now law enforcement officers redoubled their efforts to clear up the mystery.

> *... being well covered with his shield and with his lance at rest, he bore down upon them at a full gallop and fell upon the first mill that stood in his way, giving a thrust at the wing, which was whirling at such a speed that his lance was broken into bits and both horse and horseman went rolling over the plain, very much battered indeed.*

A break in the case finally came on August 2 when Adams received a penned note postmarked at Wheatland.

> *Dear Mr. Adams:*
> *When you get this letter I will be on my way to Canada. It wasn't me that shot you. The man that shot you is dead and buried. I killed him. You can find him somewhere close to Laramie Peak if you look hard enough. I may come back and finish the job I started when things quiet down a little. I hate thieves. I am sorry if you thought I was after you. That fellow said he was going to rob You but he forgot after he shot you. He shot you because he hated red hair.*
> *Yours truly,*
> *The Masked Rider.*

Less than a week later, Adams was arrested and jailed by Albany County Sheriff George Welm and his men. The mystery man's last memo proved to be the proverbial smoking gun. Authorities compared fingerprints on the note with smudges on the Rider's earlier warnings, and found the whorls matched Adams's fingertips. A specimen also was taken from a typewriter found at Wagner's ranch where Adams worked. Fred C. Lebhart, a court reporter, and W.P. Reed, a University of Wyoming professor, carefully compared it with that of the Masked Rider's typed messages. The typed materials were identical. Adding to the evidence was the discovery that the bullet fired at Atkinson was the same caliber as Adams's pistol. And there was only one bullet hole in Adams's shirt…at the exit wound. Obviously he had pressed the gun against his bare chest before pulling the trigger.

> …I am sure that this must be the work of that magician Feston, the one who robbed me of my study and my books, and who has thus changed the giants into windmills in order to deprive me of the glory of overcoming them, so great is the enmity that he bears me.

Poor Adams! Born in a period too tame for an overly imaginative boy who spent many of his waking hours reading pulp western and detective stories, he fancied himself a crusader against lawlessness. Cattle stealing and other "out of the way affairs" needed to be investigated, he later testified, because some ranchers "were doing too well" financially to be strictly honest.

The trouble, Adams confessed, started in early June 1930 when he first drew and posted warning signs trimmed with crude sketches of a cowboy's head. As far as rancher Atkinson was concerned, Adams said he never meant to hurt him. He only wanted to scare him and warn him to "quit harboring thieves." Court transcripts say Adams added, "When I thot the gang suspected me, I shot a hole in my saddle and poked another hole through my trowsers with a file." When the law caught his scent, he turned the gun on himself. "I didn't intend to do such a good job of shooting myself," he said. "I thought a little 'burning' would be enough."

On August 11, prosecutor and Albany County attorney F.K. Dukes accused Adams of breach of peace and a warrant was issued. That same day, Adams was arraigned and brought before Justice of the Peace W. H. Hayes, to whom he pleaded guilty. His sentence? A fifty-dollar fine and court costs plus thirty days in county jail. Unable to pay the fine, Adams found his time was stretched to eighty days. Working his fine off at a dollar a day, he spent much of his time standing in his cell, a magazine resting on the top tier of his bunk, still reading his favorite stories about the wild and wooly West.

So ends the tale of an imaginative young cowboy who read himself into a misadventure that created banner headlines from coast to coast. After serving his sentence, he drifted away and passed into history like Don Quixote, the fictional character his actions emulated.

> *By the world he set small store*
> *He frightened it to the core*
> *Yet somehow, by Fate's plan,*
> *Though he'd lived a crazy man,*
> *When he died he was sane once more.*

❧ SOURCES CITED ❧ Although the primary information for this story came from the Laramie, Wyoming, Justice of the Peace Criminal Docket and Albany County Sheriff's Records & Prisoner Register, the inspiration for its telling must be credited to *The Ingenious Gentleman, Don Quixote de la Mancha* by Cervantes, the great Spanish author. Nor could have Charley Adams's troubled life and fantasies have been told in such detail without the numerous newspaper stories published from July 6 through August 14, 1930, in such periodicals as the *Wheatland Times & World* and the *Sheridan Post-Enterprise*. All of these source materials may be found in the Wyoming State Archives.

This chapter first appeared, in a slightly different form, in *Wyoming Annals* (Vol. 66, Nos. 1 & 2), Spring/Summer 1994.

ᴀʟʟᴇɴ Ƭ. Ƭʀᴜᴇ

A TRUE TRIBUTE TO THE WEST

Soft light streaming through rare Tiffany stained-glass ceilings gives life to eight allegorical scenes that hang high on the grand walls of Wyoming's State Capitol where its state legislature meets. In the House Chamber, on the second floor at the east end of the gray granite building, visitors find scenes named "Trappers," "Cattlemen," "Homesteaders," and "Stage Coach." At the same level in the Senate Chamber's west wing, "Frontier Cavalry Officers," "Railroad Builders-Surveyors," "Pony Express Rider," and "Indian Chief Cheyenne" remind visitors of Wyoming's struggles to survive. The icons also prod the collective conscience of state representatives and senators who return to their desks each session to draft and pass laws that provide for the well-being, growth, and development of Wyoming.

These are the works of Allen T. (Tupper) True, who on August 17, 1917—during the administration of Acting Governor Frank L. Houx—contracted to paint the large oils on canvas for a total of $5,200. The art, True said, should serve "to honor the pioneer and to record for coming generations the picturesque phases of the West which were nowhere more adaptable than in Wyoming." Although True never lived in Cheyenne, one brother, James, became a state engineer and state highway superintendent there, and another, Henry, served a term as a Cheyenne city commissioner. Mrs. A.R. Wilson, a sister, resided in the "Magic City on the Plains" until 1954. Diemer True, a former state senator from Casper, is the artist's grand-nephew.

True perhaps is best remembered in Wyoming, however, for creating the state's famed symbol of the bronc-riding cowboy. The artist was living in Denver, Colorado, in 1934, when Dr. Lester C. Hunt, then Wyoming's secretary of state (later governor and United States senator), asked him to design a bucking horse and rider for use on Wyoming vehicle license plates. The original sketch, for which Hunt paid True seventy-five dollars, decorated the senator's office in Washington, D.C., until after Hunt's death in 1954.

Born in Colorado Springs, Colorado, on May 30, 1881, to Henry A. and Margaret Tupper True, Allen True attended the University of Denver for two years before plunging into an art career by enrolling at the prestigious Corcoran College of Art and Design in Washington, D.C. Then from 1902 to 1908, he became the pupil of the celebrated illustrator Howard Pyle, whose subdued style permanently influenced True's work. Pyle and True's great friend N.C. Wyeth led what came to be known as the Delaware School of historical illustration. Later, True studied under the famous British artist Frank Brangwyn and served as his assistant for two years in his London studio.

True first won widespread acclaim as an illustrator, with his art featured for several years in such leading magazines as *Scribner's*, *Collier's*, and *Saturday Evening Post*. But after returning to live in the Rocky Mountains, he gained perhaps even greater fame for his large wall paintings. Mostly executed in matte earth tones, blues, and greens, their subtle snatches of red, orange, and ochre pull the viewer's eye. In addition to those he painted for the Wyoming State Capitol, he also developed a series of eight epic scenes for the rotunda of the Colorado State Capitol to illustrate the history of the West and its dependence upon water. And he painted murals of historic scenes for the Missouri State Capitol in Jefferson City, served as an art consultant to the United States Reclamation Bureau, and directed the decoration and color schemes of interiors at the Hoover Dam.

True married Emma Goodman Eaton on June 3, 1915; they later divorced. At age seventy-four, the internationally acclaimed artist died at his home on November 1, 1955, after a prolonged heart illness. Four children and three grandchildren survived him.

L.C. Hunt, Wyoming's secretary of state from 1934 to 1938, admires the logo, designed by Allen True, that has decorated Wyoming's automobile license plates since 1936. (Wyoming State Archives)

❧ SOURCES CITED ❧ Allen True's artistry must be seen to be fully appreciated. That is why I visited the Wyoming State Capitol on February 8, 1996 to study the large paintings in their intended context. I also examined the Wyoming State Archives subject file concerning True and his work, including his February 9, 1917 letter to the Wyoming Capitol Commission in which he described his proposed murals and their pricing.

Most of this information about True's origins, family, and career is based upon newspaper articles published at the time of his death: "True, Denver Muralist, Dies at 74 After Long Illness," *Casper Tribune-Herald*, November 9, 1955, p. 14; "Mural Painter Dies in Denver," *Denver Post*, November 9, 1955, pp. 5–6; and "Designer of State Bucking Horse Dies," *Wyoming State Tribune*, Cheyenne, November 9, 1955, pp. 1, 11. Those especially interested in True's design of Wyoming's logo will enjoy Jean C. Gaddy's "Wyoming's Insignia: The Bucking Horse," *Wyoming Annals* (Vol. 26, No. 2), July 1954, pp. 129–136.

I also gained some background about True, his mentors, and his role in contemporary art from *The Arts in America, 19th Century* (New York: Chas. Scribner's Sons, 1969, p. 277), edited by D. Garret Wendell, Paul. F. Norton, Alan Gowans, and Joseph Butler.

This chapter first appeared, in a slightly different form, in the *Casper Star-Tribune*, February 26, 1996.

CHAPTER 4

JOHN C. THOMPSON

IN OLD WYOMING

Why is there a rather general disposition to deprecate the legis-lature? If all the wisecracks of this category were laid end to end they'd reach from the last smartaleck who made one back to the beginning of time and lap over into infinity. Forty years of reporting legislatures have seen a steady increase of the respect with which this writer regards the average earnest, honest well-meaning citizen who is representing his fellow citizen in the law making branch of the government.

THUS, FOR THE first time—on February 11, 1937—John C. Thompson expressed "One Man's Opinion" under that banner in the *Wyoming State Tribune*, the newspaper he edited.

As a Cheyenne newspaperman since the age of eighteen, Thompson had observed and reported the news for roughly forty years. But that was not enough. All along, he sensed Wyoming and its people had failed to receive the attention and recognition they deserved, and it concerned him greatly. To make sure his state's citizens and posterity would remember "the people who had accomplished things from the bottom up," the congenial but rather private journalist collected a rich trove of facts and anecdotes about their lives. Then, thanks to his sense of history, he placed their stories prominently in the newspaper for which he worked. In doing so, he enriched his readers' lives by putting the events of their time in perspective.

In addition to his skills as a writer, some say he possessed even greater gifts: the ability to cultivate invaluable news sources, ask the right questions, and accurately recall the most obscure facts. The courtly gentleman also had great empathy for his fellow man. Oh, he could be stern, aloof, and even irascible at times, but usually he saved his rancor for those who he perceived as lacking "moral fiber."

And unlike many of his firebrand competitors, Thompson chose reason rather than rhetoric to express his views. He congratulated rather than castigated. Tired of pit-bull editorializing, the public seemed to find Thompson's straight talk refreshing. They warmed to his yarns about the good ol' days like trail-worn travelers taking comfort near a friendly fire.

As he matured professionally from reporter to editor, "Charley," as a few close friends called him, spent more and more time in search of interesting individuals who had made important contributions, particularly to Thompson's new home city. In telling their tales, he evolved into a kindly mentor. And to reflect that approach, just twelve days after launching his series he retitled his column "Cheyenne, Wyoming" on February 23, 1937.

Readers discovered, within Thompson's column rule, the great strengths of Wyoming people, including honor, fidelity, self-sufficiency, honesty, fairness, and above all, a sense of equality. Those attributes came alive in his stories in such a way as to help his readers cope with and succeed in their own lives. Indeed, Thompson found that the values he cherished most transcended those who lived in the "Magic City on the Plains," and that Wyoming's history still lived within its people. With that discovery, he chose a more appropriate title for his column: "In Old Wyoming." It first appeared on July 27, 1938. In that issue he mused:

> It would be interesting to know how many men there are in Cheyenne whose careers included a period when they were carrier-boys for one or another of the several newspapers now merged in and their names perpetuated by The Tribune.

Clearly he must have recalled his own youthful start in journalism.

He was born July 15, 1879, at Harrodsburg, Kentucky. Thompson's father—also named John C.—brought the boy to Cheyenne five years later. After working as a miner and stenographer, junior Thompson launched his newspaper career in 1897 as "conductor of

John Charles Thompson (right), chats in his office at the Wyoming State Tribune *with T. Joe Cahill, Cheyenne's chief of police, circa 1942. Both men witnessed the November 20, 1903, execution of Tom Horn, the notorious cattle detective and convicted murderer.* (Beriah Thompson collection)

the Wyoming department" at the *Rocky Mountain News*, based in Denver, Colorado. Three years later he became a reporter for the *Tribune;* then in 1902 he joined the *Cheyenne Leader*, which he edited from 1908 through 1911. The following year, after a brief stint as Laramie County assessor, he returned to the *Tribune* where he worked for the next five years as a reporter.

During 1917–18, he served as Governor Frank Houx's secretary before returning two years later to the *Tribune* where he again became editor. During the next decade and a half he also served as editor of the *Tribune's* subsidiary, the *Wyoming Stockman-Farmer*.

During his long journalism career Thompson covered every major news story in Wyoming, including Tom Horn's murder trial (see chapter 11: "Killing Men Was His Specialty"), the Jackson Hole congressional investigations, the pre–World War I convict strike at the state penitentiary in Rawlins, mine disasters at Hanna, and the Teapot Dome scandal. During much of that time, he also worked as a correspondent for the *New York Times* and wrote extensively for other major newspapers and periodicals. His zeal for history also brought him an appointment to the Wyoming State Historical Landmarks Commission in 1939.

Despite his many interests and responsibilities, Thompson always carved time from a busy schedule to craft his column. "In Old Wyoming" welcomed its readers nearly every day for more than twelve years. Like strong coffee and sunrise, it seemed to offer the comfort and spirit they needed to meet their daily challenges. Not content to hide it on an inside page, Thompson let his writings compete on Page One with the hard news of crime, death, and taxes. Rarely did he allow it to be pushed from the newspaper by anything short of a major disaster or nations at war.

The stress and long hours imposed by the rigors of his business, the debilitating effects of nearly ten years of cardiovascular disease, his wife Della Mae's heart attack, and the tragic death of his son Edward in 1947, however, finally took their toll. Thompson's once bright torch slowly faded to a glow like the embered tip of his ever-present cigarette. "In Old Wyoming" went to print for the last time on Friday, July 14, 1950, with Thompson's wearied words tagging slowly behind some lengthy introductory quotes by characters in Virginia Cole Trenholm's *Footprints on the Frontier*.

About a year and a half later—on February 8, 1952—words finally failed him, and Thompson's life ended.

❧ SOURCES CITED ❧ Many of Mr. Thompson's relatives, friends, and associates kindly shared recollections about his life and times with me. Folks like T. Raymond Cahalane, Don Clair, and Pat Sullivan Larsen gave me personalized insight into his career and journalistic ethics. And surviving family members such as Beriah "Bill" Thompson and Shelby Thompson generously helped me, with their memories and records, to reconstruct the Thompson family history.

Although I found the best summary of his life in the obituary published in the *Wyoming State Tribune* on February 8, 1952, I also read most of the editorials and feature stories that John C. Thompson wrote about Wyoming's past as well as his own times and the characters he shared them with. Those may be found in the *Wyoming State Tribune* and *Wyoming Stockman-Farmer* from February 11, 1937, to February 8, 1952.

This chapter first appeared, in a slightly different form, in *Wyoming Annals* (Vol. 65, No. 4), Winter 1993-1994.

CHAPTER 5

Heart Mountain Internees

STITCHES OF TRUTH

Her deft fingers sew small jade knots on dwarfed pines that wend their way along the pale muslin and up the side of Heart Mountain toward its grey Fuji-like peak. Bright pink buds, bound by green and gold leaves, sprout from nearby tight stitches, where stems of rough brown threads stretch for the sun's first light. And near the front door of a deep-hued hut, grass of green strands spike the dark earth.

Is it the scene of a dream...a memory...the wish of an unknown artist? It may be all of these, but the Asian woman's needle, perhaps blinded by tears, fails to tell the whole truth.

Seventy-four days after Japan's December 7, 1941, attack on Pearl Harbor, President Franklin D. Roosevelt ordered 100,000 people of Japanese ancestry—two-thirds were American citizens—from their homes on the Pacific coast to ten relocation points in the interior of the United States. Government authorities built one of these centers near Heart Mountain, between Cody and Powell in Wyoming.

At a cost of more than five million dollars, the Army Corps of Engineers erected more than 560 barracks on 46,000 acres of public domain in the shadow of a rocky butte that overlooks miles of windswept sage. Each 20-foot by 100-foot structure contained six rooms, none larger than a two-car garage. Tarpaper covered the wood-sheathed walls. In fact, officials boasted that one of those "apartment" buildings could be built within fifty-eight minutes. A barbed-wire fence, fanned each night by high-beam searchlights and guarded by nine armed soldiers, surrounded the camp.

The Heart Mountain relocation center, between Cody and Powell in Wyoming, was one of ten such internment facilities built by the U.S. government to house people of Japanese ancestry who were living in the United States after the Japanese military attacked Pearl Harbor. (Wyoming State Archives)

The internees began to arrive on August 13, 1942, with each family, regardless of size, assigned to a single room with cots, mattresses, blankets, a bucket, and a broom. A makeshift curtain gave scant privacy. The barracks had no running water, and the community showers and laundries were far removed in separate buildings. The stalls of the public toilets had no doors. Heart Mountain's population, which grew to more than 12,000, had but eight bathtubs and twelve showers in which to bathe. As winter came, authorities installed coal-burning stoves, but many families at first had to shovel dirt against the walls to block the drafts beneath their floors. Insulation came later, as did the construction of a recreation hall, mess hall, hospital, and school.

Despite such harsh conditions, the Japanese learned to make do. One woman, for example, made a kitchen sink out of two five-gallon salad-oil cans salvaged from the mess hall. She put them side by side, using one for clean water and one for waste. A peanut-butter

This embroidery is a contemporary example of an ancient Japanese art form. Although it depicts Heart Mountain and the World War II internment camp, some believe the unknown artist was recalling her native land's sacred Mount Fuji when she created this piece. (Wyoming State Museum)

can with a wooden handle served as a dipper. And a coal bin—furnished with a card table and chairs built from orange crates and draped with handmade slipcovers—became a "den."

Despite a ban on private enterprise by the inmates, a few "prospered" by selling their crafts at religious festivals and bazaars in the compound. At one such event, Jean E. Cooper, who taught at Heart Mountain during 1944–45, bought the wonderful bit of embroidery that illustrates this story.

Despite hard times suffered by the Japanese inmates at the grim complex, those like Estelle Ishigo stoically tried to find their futures while seeking reasons for their fate. In a story titled "Lone Heart Mountain," which tells of her life there, she wrote, "Gathered close into ourselves and imprisoned at the foot of the mountain, we searched its gaunt face for the mystery of our destiny."

The Heart Mountain Relocation Center closed on November 15, 1945.

❧ SOURCES CITED ❧ To fully appreciate the lovely, intricately stitched art that first focused my attention on the Heart Mountain Relocation Center and those forced to live there, readers may ask at the Wyoming State Museum to see artifact #85.12.1 and its accession records.

I also interviewed by phone Jean E. Cooper of Cheyenne, who worked as a teacher at the Heart Mountain Relocation Center during 1944–45. She bought the splendid embroidery at that time for a since-forgotten price from a female detainee, and later donated it to the museum.

For details concerning the camp's origin, construction, and daily life there, readers may wish to review the following articles: Doreen Chaky's "Wyoming's Ghosts," *Wyoming Rural Electric News*, February 1971, as well as J. Randle Mood's "History of the Meeteetse Mercantile," *Annals of Wyoming* (Vol. 49, No. 2), Fall 1997, pp. 274–277, 284; "Heart Mountain Relocation Center Was World War II Home for 11,000 Japanese," *Powell* (Wyoming) *Tribune*, July 1, 1976, pp. 1D-2D; and "Inside Wyoming, Heart Mountain Recollections," which appeared in two issues of *Annals of Wyoming*: Vol. 60, No. 1 (Spring 1988), pp. 45–49; and Vol. 61, No. 1 (Spring 1989), pp. 47–54. See, too, Douglas W. Nelson's *Heart Mountain: The History of an American Concentration Camp* (Madison, WI: The State Historical Society of Wisconsin for the Department of History, University of Wisconsin, 1976). Estelle Ishigo's poignant words can be found in "Lone Heart Mountain," published in the aforementioned issue of the *Powell Tribune*, p. 2D.

This chapter first appeared, in a slightly different form, in the *Casper Star-Tribune*, September 15, 1996.

CHAPTER 6

FRANK MEANEA

"MEANIE" MADE THE BEST

*I wish it understood that I make a specialty of stock saddle trees,
and spare no pains or expense in making them as good as they
can possibly be made… nothing but the best of everything.*

—from F.A. Meanea's 1922 saddle shop catalog

THE CHOICE, HAND-TOOLED leather art of Frank Meanea is a treat for the eyes of those who fancy fine design. It is sweet, too, to the noses of those who savor the subtle scent of fine-grained, well-oiled cowhide. But to many an old-time ranch hand, whose life, limbs, and livelihood depended upon a firm, form-fitting seat strapped to the back of a cow pony, a "Meanie-made" saddle came as a gift from God.

Francis Augustis Meanea found life on December 16, 1849, near Lexington, Missouri, where he shared a home with his French parents, a brother, and a sister. Eighteen years later, when the Union Pacific pushed its steel rails west, Frank, as most called him, launched a career that won him fame as one of the West's best craftsmen. Since much of the rail grade work relied on teams of oxen and mules the toll on harness and wagons proved great, so the young man started a small repair business. The following fall (1868), at the Bear River railhead near Wyoming's western border, Frank received a letter from his uncle E.L. Gallatin, one of the first and finest saddlers in the Colorado Territory. Gallatin wrote that he and his partner planned to start a branch firm in Cheyenne. So at age nineteen, the nephew agreed to manage the new Gallatin & Gallup shop which opened in a one-story frame house at 218 West Seventeenth Street. The front room served as the center for saddlery

Frank Meanea, who would become one of the West's premier saddle-makers, launched his career at age nineteen by managing his uncle E.L. Gallatin's leather and tack shop at 218 West Seventeenth Street in Cheyenne, Wyoming. (Wyoming State Archives)

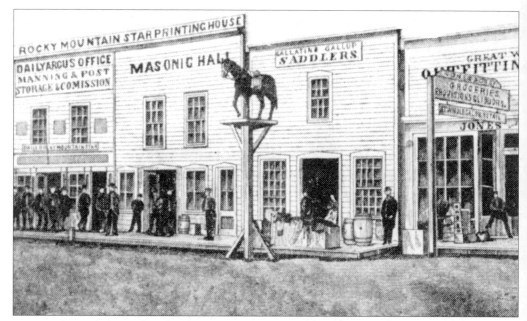

A wooden pony found its home on a pedestal in front of Gallatin & Gallup Saddlers after Frank Meanea agreed to manage the shop when it opened in 1869. Meanea, who made, repaired, and sold tack at the front of the building, lived with his widowed mother in a room at the rear. (Wyoming State Archives)

and sales, while the rear provided living quarters for Frank and his widowed mother. The venture became so successful that in 1876 Frank bought the store, expanding it several years later into a new two-story brick building on the original site.

Although he and his staff specialized in saddles, they believed firmly that "If it can be made in leather, we do it." And to prove that point, they also made harness and a variety of items to adorn the rider, including spur straps, belts, holsters, and chaps. At the peak of his career, to meet the thriving demand from customers in nearly every state as well as Europe, Australia, Russia, South Africa, Canada, and Mexico, Frank employed twenty-two master craftsmen and a host of clerks, bookkeepers, and other support staff.

Yet the artisan always gave his personal attention to all repair work brought to his shop because he took great pride in doing even the smallest job as well as possible.

With the influx of sodbusters and the drop in travel on horse-back and in wagons, the saddle trade tapered off as the decades passed. The most telling blow to Frank's firm came about 1911 with the advent of automobiles, but still he found customers. Finally, in 1927, after about forty-five years at the same site, he moved the F.A. Meanea Saddle Shop to a smaller building at 320 West Seventeenth Street.

His wife, Kate (Bolander), died in 1913, but their adopted child Byrde survived her to wed W.J. Holnholz. On November 22, 1928, the world-renowned saddler died at age seventy-nine while visiting his brother's family in Golden, Colorado. He found peace in his family's plot at Lakeview Cemetery in Cheyenne.

❧ SOURCES CITED ❧ Those interested in Frank Meanea's craft can find samples of his work in the most prominent Old West museums throughout the high plains and Rocky Mountain states. To better understand his artistry, however, I drove to the Pine Bluffs, Wyoming, shop of my talented friend Jim Darden, who not only teaches how to make saddles, but makes and repairs them as well. As I touched and viewed some of Meanea's fine works in the collection there, Jim explained and helped me to appreciate the special quali-ties of Meanea's art.

To learn more about saddle making and about Meanea's life, the reader may turn to three articles in the *Annals of Wyoming:* Nora Dunn's "Frank A. Meanea, Pioneer Saddler," (Vol. 26, No. 1), 1954, pp. 25–32; A.S. "Bud" Gillespie's "Saddles," (Vol. 34, No. 2), 1962, p. 215, and G.W. Rosentrater's "My Cowboy Experi-ences in the 1890s," (Vol. 37, No. 2), 1964, p. 227. Also of interest is "Meanea Saddles: Light & Heavy Harness, Bits, Spurs, Ropes, Chaps, Bridles, Hackamores, etc.," Catalog #19, 1922, on file at the Wyoming State Archives.

This chapter first appeared, in a slightly different form, in the *Casper Star-Tribune*, April 14, 1996.

CHAPTER 7

JUAN MENCHACA

MENCHACA MADE MINIATURES

I T IS A BIRD'S-EYE view of an 1880s spring roundup near Chugwater, Wyoming. Cows seem to graze sweet sage while 'pokes sear a calf's taut flank with the outfit's brand. So real is the scene that some spectators wince at the critter's silent cries as ghost smoke curls from its burned hide. And near a chuck wagon where "Cookie" stirs his stew, the sight of a dull black coffeepot over a campfire makes the mouth water for its rich, strong brew.

But the brain deceives. There is no taste, no sound, no smell. And if you try to touch the small figures, a guard will remind you the three-dimensional setting is a Wyoming State Museum diorama. Its sculptured figures and lifelike details blend indistinguishably with the realistic painted background. This is no snapped-together kit of plastic parts. Rather, it is one of famed artist Juan Menchaca's few hand-carved and hand-painted works in Wyoming.

Born March 8, 1910, as the eldest of Frank and Eutilia (Vargas) Menchaca's six children, Juan spent his first years on their family farm near Fort Worth, Texas. Following an elementary and high school education, his natural artistic talent earned him pocket money and acclaim with murals he painted in churches and restaurants. That raw skill gained the attention of faculty at the Texas School of Fine Art, where Menchaca enrolled, trading janitorial help for lessons in drawing, painting, and sculpture.

After completing art school, he first created scenes of the Trinity River, but soon turned to portraiture. When the small commissions he earned did not provide a livelihood, he joined a friend and spent a summer in Wyoming, topping beets in fields near Wheatland.

Juan Menchaca, although perhaps best known for his dioramas depicting specific historical events, began his career in the fine arts, painting oil portraits of celebrated pioneers as well as the flora and fauna of the Old West. Here he recreates the majestic bison on canvas at his Lakeview, Colorado, home studio in April 1994. (Mark Junge)

Dazzled by the beauty of the Rocky Mountains, he went south to Denver where he met Robert Graham, an artist with a studio near the Colorado State Capitol. In return for mixing paints, cleaning brushes, and sweeping floors, Menchaca learned Graham's sophisticated art techniques.

In 1935, Menchaca returned to Texas and married, then moved with his wife to their new home in Denver. During a visit to the nearby Colorado State Museum of History, he met its director who hired him to do portraits of celebrated pioneers, then later assigned him to paint backgrounds for dioramas. By 1965, as he gained experience and prominence, Wyoming State Museum officials hired him—during a year-long leave of absence from his work in Colorado—to create the "Spring Round-up" diorama. He

Menchaca's diorama of an 1880s roundup includes models of twenty-eight head of cattle, ten horses, nine cowboys, and a chuck wagon. (Wyoming State Museum)

built it in his Denver garage after lengthy studies of historic sketches and photos.

He subsequently worked for the National Cowboy Hall of Fame in Oklahoma City before retiring in 1977 to his home in Lakewood, Colorado.

❧ SOURCES CITED ❧ After studying Menchaca's marvelous "Spring Round-up" diorama at the Wyoming State Museum, I sought out two exceptional documents before writing this article. They are available, respectively, at the Wyoming State Museum and the Wyoming State Archives: the accession records for Menchaca's diorama (artifact #99.49) and Mark Junge's transcribed April 12, 1994, interview with Menchaca at the artist's home in Lakewood, Colorado.

This chapter first appeared, in a slightly different form, in the *Casper Star-Tribune*, May 12, 1996.

CHAPTER 8

Thomas Molesworth

MOLESWORTH FURNITURE, THE BEST IN THE WEST

THE WILDNESS OF THE West grabs the eye of those who enter the great log cabin. Captured in textile, thunderbirds soar across the woolen backs of chairs. On a bedroom door, a bandy-legged gunfighter challenges those who enter, while etched Indian maidens and elk seem to call from the routed surfaces of rough-hewn wood furniture.

That Glenwood, Colorado, ranch scene, featured in a 1989 *House & Garden* article, helped make famous Thomas Canada Molesworth, who had completed the project in 1935 as one of his grandest commissions for prominent New York stockbroker George Sumers and his family. Molesworth, a furniture maker extraordinaire, gained prominence from the 1930s through the 1950s by populariz-ing the "western craftsman" genre of popular decorative arts.

Born in Coronado, Kansas, on September 28, 1890, as the youngest son of preacher Albert M. Molesworth and his wife Emma (Childers), the boy soon displayed unusual artistic talent. So much so, in fact, that in 1908 he enrolled in the prestigious Art Institute of Chicago. Family financial problems the following year, however, forced him to leave school.

After working briefly for a local furniture firm and a bank, he enlisted in the United States Marines and served a stint in France during World War I. He subsequently joined his parents, who had moved to Billings, Montana. Young Molesworth managed a furni-ture company there, marrying LaVerne M. Johnston in 1917. Fourteen years and two children later, Molesworth announced "he'd rather die broke than work for someone else," so he moved

Tom Molesworth poses astride his horse in the driveway entry to his factory at the west end of Cody, circa 1950. When his first factory building burned to the ground the night before it was to be occupied, Cody townspeople and service clubs immediately rallied to clean up and rebuild. This set of log buildings is still in use as a motel. (Mr. and Mrs. Lee Molesworth collection, Ventura, CA)

his family south to Cody, Wyoming, where he opened the Shoshone Furniture Store.

There the craftsman-designer first fashioned interiors of such rugged zest they fulfilled city slickers' fantasies of a home on the range. The most obscure details in his celebrated roomscapes bore his imprint: doorstops, fireplace screens, gin-rummy scorecards, and drink coasters. Molesworth draped windows with horsehide curtains; he scattered Navajo rugs over floors and banisters. And the polished burl legs and fine, fringed leathers of his cowboy furniture marked each interior as a Molesworth.

His success spread and his clients, ranging from neighbors to celebrities, offered him projects from dude ranches to luxury liners,

Molesworth-designed furniture, on display in the "Governor's Den" at the Historic Governor's Mansion in Cheyenne, is as functional as it is romantic. The Indian paintbrush, Wyoming's state flower, is punch-embroidered on the backs of the upholstered chairs. The shade of the fanciful wagon lamp is made of lambskin; the floor lamp's is unborn calfskin. (Wyoming State Museum)

from rumpus rooms to President Dwight Eisenhower's den. He incorporated into his western chic settings the themes and designs of such famed western artists as Charlie Russell, Hans Kleiber, and E.W. Gollings. Italian artisans laid terrazzo tiles to form his scenes of cockfighting, flamenco dancing, and bronco-busting. German blacksmiths forged chandeliers with stampeding iron bison and strap hinges in the shape of horned owls. Molesworth's designs were truly world-class.

Following his death on July 19, 1977, at his home at Scottsdale, Arizona, his family returned his ashes to Wyoming, where they scattered them on Cedar Mountain near Cody.

⚘ SOURCES CITED ⚘ Inspired by a visit to the Old Governor's Mansion in Cheyenne where a special roomscape displays a selection of Molesworth furnishings, I turned to the following articles in order to better understand his life and art: Margot Guralnick's "Colorado Cabin Fever," *House & Garden*, December 1989, pp. 158–167; Michael M. Thomas's "In the Shadow of the Rockies: Renewing the Historic Cody Ranch in Wyoming," *Architectural Digest*, September 1987, pp. 150–155; and his obituary, "Thomas Molesworth Dies," *Cody* (Wyoming) *Enterprise*, August 3, 1977.

The *Sweetwater Ranch* catalog of western furniture, as well as *Interior West: The Craft and Style of Thomas Molesworth*, the exhibition catalog produced in September 1989 by Wally Reber and Paul Fees for the Buffalo Bill Historical Center in Cody, Wyoming, also provided insight into the designer's art.

This chapter first appeared, in a slightly different form, in the *Casper Star-Tribune*, April 28, 1996.

CHAPTER 9

JACKSON SUNDOWN

EARTH LEFT BY SETTING SUN

THE SPLENDIDLY HAND-SEWN buckskin shirt trimmed with bright bits of glass emerges like a butterfly as the Wyoming State Museum's curator pulls the artifact from its plastic "cocoon." The front of the garment has a yoke of red cloth while panels of black and pink beads on a light-blue background drape the shoulders. The sleeves, too, have beadwork panels of the same design. Ermine skins, some with brass bells attached, hang from the shoulders, the beaded sleeves, and the panels on the back.

As the young woman carefully lays the shirt on the table, she explains that the well-worn garment, with its mysterious symbols, almost always piques her visitors' curiosity. They also tend to spur the inquisitive to learn more about the life of Waaya-tona-toesits-kahn ("Earth Left by Setting Sun"), the Indian cowboy who wore it.

Best known in the white man's world by his anglicized name, Jackson Sundown was born in 1863 in a tipi under the big sky that blanketed the Montana Territory. From early childhood, the nephew of Chief Joseph rode his own Appaloosa pony, having learned by watching the superb horsemanship of his Nez Perce tribe's warriors. His idyllic childhood ended, however, at age eleven when he and two other Indian boys hid under bison robes as United States Army troops, led by General O.O. Howard, made a surprise pre-dawn attack on their encampment on August 9, 1877. When the military set fire to their tent, the youngsters escaped.

Following that "Battle of the Big Hole," young Sundown and his people fled toward Canada to enlist the aid of Sioux in refuge there. But on a snowy September 30 on Bear Paw Mountain, the Army cavalry

Jackson Sundown, a Nez Perce cowboy from Culdesac, Idaho, was a nephew of Chief Joseph. He won the famed 1916 Roundup bronc-riding championship in Pendleton, Oregon, making a sensational ride on Angel. He was fifty-three years old at the time. (Howdy Shell Photos, Pendleton, OR)

again swept down on the cold and exhausted natives. The lad eluded his enemy this time by hanging from the side of his horse so that the soldiers thought it had no rider. Wounded in the fray, and without blankets or food, he nevertheless continued north, eventually reaching the safety of Chief Sitting Bull's camp just inside Canada.

Sundown returned to the United States about two years later and settled on the Flathead Indian Reservation in Montana where in 1894 he married a woman named Pew-lo-sap, also known as Annie.

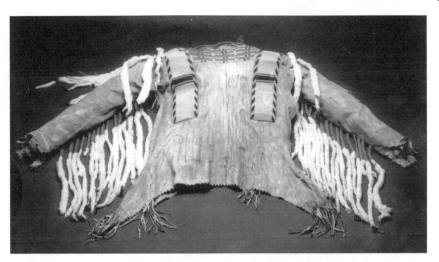

Sundown's war shirt, split on both sides to facilitate movement, goes beyond ethnic fashion; it carries symbols with ceremonial meaning. The set of shoulder bands customarily were bestowed by the tribe for an individual's valor in its defense. The fringe of ermine skins also signifies the warrior's battle prowess. Tipped with bells and feathers, the cured hides danced with each gesture of the arms or tugs of the breeze. (Wyoming State Museum)

Following the birth of three daughters, the couple moved their family six years later to Culdesac, Idaho, only to divorce in 1905. Meanwhile, Sundown honed his bronc-busting skills and won a championship belt at the 1912 Border Days Rodeo at Grangeville. The following year he remarried, this time to Wap-shi-lai, or Cecilia, a Nez Perce widow with two children. They subsequently built a cabin on Mission Creek between Lapwai and Culdesac.

Then, in 1916, Sundown entered the bucking horse event at the prestigious Pendleton Roundup in Oregon. The day of the finals, a capacity crowd hushed as the lean, six-foot rider, clad in a bright shirt and shaggy orange angora chaps, climbed aboard the saddled back of a huge bay named Angel. When a waddy jerked the blindfold from the outlaw bronc's eyes, the animal immediately tried to jar loose the long black braids tied beneath his rider's chin. According to a witness, "Angel bent almost in two, vainly trying to unseat his rider" as members of the throng rose to their feet yelling, "Sundown... Sundown... Ride 'em, Sundown!" Soon after the timekeeper's pistol signaled the end of the ride, rodeo officials crowned the fifty-three-year-old cowboy World Champion Saddle Bronc Rider, the first American Indian so honored.

During the next seven years, Sundown worked as a handyman and helped train horses at a ranch on the Salmon River. On December 18, 1923, the sixty-year-old died of pneumonia at Jacques Spur, Idaho. He is buried in the local Slickpoo Mission Church cemetery.

❧ SOURCES CITED ❧ Jackson Sundown's colorful Nez Perce war shirt and leggings, which were obtained sometime prior to 1990 by the Wyoming State Museum, are described in detail in the Museum's accession records and curatorial notes for artifact #21.1.27.3c.

For specific details of his life, however, the reader will be best served by the following articles: Rowena Alcorn and D. Gordon's "Indian Legend on Horseback," *Frontier Times* (Vol. 45, No. 2), 1966, pp. 22–23, 48; "Jackson Sundown, Nez Perce Indian, Rides to World Fame," *Idaho County Free Press*, Grangeville, ID, June 1976, p. 1; and Mohsin Askar's "Those Who Saw Jackson Sundown Ride Never Forgot It," *Lewiston* (Idaho) *Tribune*, May 6, 1990. The *Lewiston Morning Tribune* also marked his death with "Memorial Set for Sundown," May 12, 1967, and "Nez Perce Tribe Honors Member With Marker," May 14, 1967.

The following books also comment on Sundown's exciting life: Thomas E. Mails's *The Mystic Warriors of the Plains* (Garden City, NJ: Doubleday & Co., Inc., 1972), pp. 232–344; Omie Smith and Lorena Miller's *Tsceminicum* (Lewiston, ID: Idaho Writers League, Printcraft Print Co. 1963), pp. 81–83; Erwin N. Thompson's *Historic Resource Study, Spalding Area, Nez Perce National Historical Park* (Denver: National Park Service, 1972), p. 183; Fr. Michael M. O'Malley's memoir, *Flocks That I Watched* (Spokane: Gonzaga University Press, 1971), pp. 55–57; and Ken Kesey with Ken Babb's *The Last Go Round* (New York: Penguin Books, 1994).

This chapter first appeared, in a slightly different form, in the *Casper Star-Tribune*, May 25, 1996.

CHAPTER 10

ELLEN "CATTLE KATE" WATSON

JUDGE ONLY AFTER WALKING IN HER MOCCASINS

ELLEN WATSON and her fourteen-year-old live-in helper John Lee DeCorey sauntered down the sunny bank of Horse Creek near its confluence with the Sweetwater River. There, at a friendly Shoshone Indian camp, she bought and donned a pair of exquisitely beaded moccasins.

Later that morning—Saturday, July 20, 1889—"Ella" and the boy returned across a hay meadow to the homestead on which she had filed a claim sixteen months earlier. As they approached her new log cabin, they discovered Ella's neighbor Albert J. Bothwell and five other prominent cattlemen—Tom (de Soleil) Sun, John H. Durbin, Robert M. Galbraith, Robert B. Connor, and M. Earnest McLean—tearing down her barbed-wire fence and scattering her cattle. During the ensuing scuffle, the men accused the twenty-eight-year-old woman of stealing their livestock, then forced her into Sun's buggy.

Traveling about a mile north, they also seized James Averell, Ella's good friend and perhaps her lover or husband, near his post office–store. Four miles farther at Spring Canyon, near the famed Independence Rock, the assailants stopped and forced Watson and Averell upon a boulder. After noosing the couple's necks to a pitch pine, the cattlemen unceremoniously pushed them into space. As Ella danced to death at the end of the rope, her new buckskin and rawhide moccasins fell into the tall grass beneath her flailing feet.

Witnesses to their abduction—DeCorey and another boy named Gene Crowder—rode to Averell's store and told Frank Buchanan, who pursued the killers. Failing that, he started a fifty-mile trip to Casper in search of the law, but got lost during the night. At three A.M., Buchanan found himself at Tex Healy's homestead. Healy rode on to Casper later that morning, arriving at about noon. In the sheriff's absence, undersheriff Phil Watson (no relation to Ella) promptly organized a posse, and acting coroner Dr. Joe Benson swore in a coroner's jury.

At daybreak the next day, Benson and members of his jury began riding with undersheriff Watson's posse toward the Sweetwater.

Arriving after midnight, they camped and ate supper before going in search of the bodies that still hung from the pine tree. When they found the macabre tableau later that morning, witnesses said the corpses "swayed to and fro by a gentle breeze which wafted the sweet odor of modest prairie flowers across the plain. The faces were discolored and shrunken tongues hung from between their swollen lips, while a film had gathered over the bulging eyes and the unnatural position of the limbs completed the frightful picture."

After cutting down the bodies and placing them in pine boxes that friends had made while awaiting the posse, Doctor Benson convened a formal inquest which concluded that Bothwell, Sun, Durbin, Galbraith, Connor, and McLean had caused the hangings. Although the law subsequently caught and brought the accused to court, justice failed to prevail. Instead, a combination of effective spin control by the Wyoming Stock Growers Association, adverse media coverage, and public prejudice successfully branded Ella and Jim as rustlers. A *Cheyenne Daily Leader* editorial typified the prevailing opinion at the time:

Let Justice Be Done

The lynching of the man and woman on the Sweetwater may be deplorable. All resorts to lynch law are deplorable in a country governed by laws, but when the law shows itself powerless and inactive, when justice is lame and halting, when there is failure to convict on down-right proofs, it is not in the nature of enterprising western men to sit idly by and have their cattle stolen and slaughtered under their very noses.

Ellen Watson, aka "Cattle Kate," may be the most misunderstood woman in western history. While many people still swear she earned her keep by selling stolen cattle that she had earned with her favors, her supporters declare her a brave pioneer who made her way as a wife, rancher, and homesteader. (Wyoming State Archives)

It is easy for an editor sitting in the security of his sanctum in Denver or Salt Lake to work himself into a condition of maudlin sentimentality over this particular lynching but we have noticed that these same editors never submit very gracefully to any imposition practiced upon themselves.

THE LEADER *believes in upholding the right, whether it is on the side of the corporation or the individual. While there is no doubt that the Stock Growers Association once carried things with a high hand in Wyoming... this is no justification for the private individuals now to plunder companies that have never done them any harm.*

Born July 2, 1861, near Arran Lake in Ontario, Canada, as the first of Thomas and Frances Watson's ten children, Ella accompanied her family in a covered wagon to Cora, Kansas. Soon thereafter they moved a few miles east to what became Lebanon.

By age eighteen, blue-eyed, auburn-haired Ella was buxom and big-boned, about five foot eight and 165 pounds. It was a hardy woman who married William A. Pickell, Jr., but she left the alcoholic farmer two years later because of his alleged abuse and infidelity. Footloose and fancy-free following her divorce, she strayed north to Red Cloud, Nebraska, then Denver, and on to Cheyenne in Wyoming Territory. Later, after moving west to Rawlins in Carbon County, she met and, though some debate this issue, she may have married Averell. Their alleged illicit doings would make them the stuff of Wyoming legend.

Although that relationship and their lives came to an end some three years later with the ranchers' double-noose ceremony, their notoriety—particularly that of "Cattle Kate"—lives on.

Instead of marking an end to their tragic story, the couple's demise, only one year before Wyoming became a state, launched an epic tale that still stirs controversy about the only woman hanged in Wyoming Territory. It also evokes near endless questions about her alleged past as "Cattle Kate" and her role as mistress of what enemies dubbed as Averell's "hog ranch."

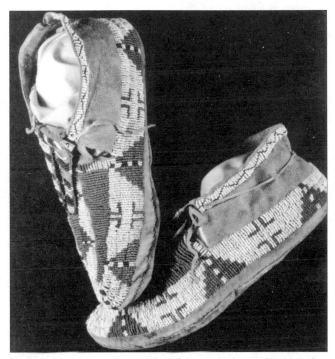

Ella's Shoshone-made moccasins were found beneath the pitch pine where assassins lynched the couple near Independence Rock. (Wyoming State Museum)

And though the law caught and brought the accused assassins to court, friends succeeded in acquitting them by branding Watson and Averell as "rustlers." Facts, however, fail to support that accusation. On the contrary, evidence suggests the strong-willed, ambitious Ella's only crime was homesteading with Jim a total of 480 acres of lush, spring-fed grassland that Bothwell coveted and where he had freely grazed his livestock until the couple arrived on the scene.

So what may we learn from this case? Who are we to believe? Did Ella, as her nemeses said, earn her keep as a whore? And did she, as they claimed, take stolen livestock in pay? Or did those who coveted the couple's homesteads murder the pair, hoping to reclaim the water and grass for their herds that once had roamed there?

We may never know for sure. But as vile as the sins of Watson and Averell are said to have been, many agree that the pair must have paid their price by now. As for their enemies, well, there are more than a few who say the hounds of hell have yet to catch their prey.

⊱ SOURCES CITED ⊱ Although western libraries seem to teem with books about the saga of "Cattle Kate" and Jim Averell, I found nothing quite so fascinating as the primary sources, copies of which are on file at the Wyoming State Archives. These include Carbon County District Court Coroner's Inquest records for James Averell and Ellen Watson, July 23, 1889; the Carbon County District Court Criminal Case Files #253, #258, and #260, July 25, 1889; and Carbon County District Court Probate Case Files, #503 for Ella Watson and #504 for James Averell.

But perhaps the most poignant primary source items are the Shoshone moccasins that fell from Ella's substantial feet during her death throes. As artifact #25.8.0 a&b they and their accession files may be seen and inspected at the Wyoming State Museum.

As for secondary sources, perhaps the best is George Hufsmith's superb *The Wyoming Lynching of Cattle Kate, 1889* (Glendo, WY: High Plains Press, 1993). Other informative books and articles include Daniel J. Meschter's *Sweetwater Sunset* (Wenatchee, WA: privately published, 1996), Sharon Leigh's "Ella Watson: Rustler or Homesteader" *Wyoming Annals* (Vol. 64, No. 3/4), Summer/Fall 1992, pp. 49–56, and "The Watson Woman," *Laramie* (Wyoming) *Boomerang*, September 23, 1889, p. 5.

This chapter first appeared, in a slightly different form, in the *Casper Star-Tribune*, July 14, 1996.

CHAPTER 11

TOM HORN

KILLING MEN WAS HIS SPECIALTY

EARLY IN JANUARY 1886, the United States Cavalry chased the fierce Geronimo and his Apache band across Arizona and some two hundred miles into Mexico. That pursuit ended on a moonless night when Tom Horn, the soldiers' civilian guide and interpreter, and his native trackers led the troops to their prey on a crag about forty miles southeast of Nacori Chico, Sonora. Demoralized, Geronimo sent word through Horn that he and his people would surrender the following morning.

But at 7 A.M. the next day—January 11—the cavalry's sentries warned their fog-wrapped camp that "soldiers" approached. Assuming the visitors to be comrades, the guards ran forward shouting greetings only to be met with a hail of bullets from about one hundred and thirty Mexican irregular troops who, the Americans swore, wanted to steal their horses and gear.

Horn said he heard attack orders from the Latinos' leader "as plainly as I could hear [commander] Captain [Emmet] Crawford's who stood beside me." Despite Horn's cries in Spanish, identifying himself and his compatriots as "friends of Mexico," the enemies fired their guns for nearly twenty-five more minutes before an assassin's bullet splattered Crawford's brains on nearby rocks. "I was halfway down meeting the Mexicans and was out in the opening," Horn recalled. "I said, 'We are American soldiers, and the Indians here are soldiers, too.'" One of the attackers immediately responded by shooting the fleshy part of Horn's upper left arm.

As the forces fought to a draw, Geronimo and his tribe vanished into the brush, only to be captured with Horn's aid the following

Tom Horn, in Judge T. Blake Kennedy's words, was "tall, a trifle round-shouldered, and had a black, beady eye which was intensely piercing." (Wyoming State Archives)

year. But then the daring interpreter's life took a tragic turn that first brought him to Wyoming, then put his head in a noose.

Born November 21, 1860, on a farm near Memphis, Missouri, Tom gained life as the fourth of Thomas and Mary Ann (Miller) Horn's eight children. Running away from home in the summer of 1873 after a beating by his father, the thirteen-year-old worked his way west through Kansas and New Mexico. His odyssey of odd jobs temporarily stopped the following year when the United States Army hired him as an interpreter for a Fifth Cavalry unit stationed in Arizona. After ten years of service with the military, Horn again hit the trail, plying a variety of trades. Finally, in the winter of 1891–92, evidence suggests he came to Wyoming and worked for a time as a cowpuncher at the Swan Land and Cattle Company near Chugwater.

Although many debate the true course of Horn's final trail, most believe he last worked as a "cattle detective" for the Wyoming Stock Growers Association, a role that entailed scaring real and aspiring rustlers as well as killing those who ignored his warnings. That career crashed, however, in January 1902, when Horn drunkenly bragged that the murder of fourteen-year-old Willie Nickell was "the best shot that I ever made and the dirtiest trick I ever done." The boy had died the previous July 18 of gunshots fired from ambush near a gate on his parents' ranch near Iron Mountain. Many still believe that the cattlemen's hired gun mistakenly killed the lad instead of Willie's cantankerous sheep-raising father, Kels.

Despite Horn's later claim of innocence, authorities arrested, tried, and convicted him for that crime.

Horn executed himself by Wyoming's "no-fault" lynching method on November 20, 1903, in the Laramie County Jail courtyard at Cheyenne. Following the sheriff's instructions, the noosed Horn stepped upon an ingeniously constructed mechanical trap in the floor of the gallows. Its timed-delay release, triggered by a water-powered counterweight system, dropped him to his death.

Family and friends buried him soon thereafter in Boulder, Colorado.

❧ SOURCES CITED ❧ Captain Emmet Crawford is a paternal great uncle of mine, and I recall that from my near infancy, my grandmother shared with me tales of his many heroic exploits. Inspired by such tales, I later spent several years compiling an in-depth chronology of his life. And that, in turn, helped me locate countless primary documents at the Arizona State Historical Society in Tucson, the Nebraska State Historical Society in Lincoln, and the Wyoming State Archives in Cheyenne. I also inspected at the Wyoming State Museum the handcuffs that Tom Horn may have worn following his arrest for the murder of fourteen-year-old Willie Nickell, and a horsehair lariat that he crafted while serving time for that crime. A careful review of the respective accession records for those artifacts—#39.14.1 and #20.45.5—also is recommended for the student of Horn's life.

As the most serious and credible secondary sources I recommend Horn's autobiography, *Life of Tom Horn: Government Scout & Interpreter, Written by Himself* (Norman, OK: University of Oklahoma Press, 1964) as well as Chip Carlson's superb trilogy on the subject, *Tom Horn: "Killing Men Is My Specialty"* (Cheyenne: Bear Corral, 1991), *Joe LeFors: "I Slickered Tom Horn…"* (Cheyenne: Bear Corral, 1995), and *Tom Horn: Blood on the Moon* (Glendo, WY: High Plains Press, 2001).

This chapter first appeared, in a slightly different form, in the *Casper Star-Tribune*, March 2, 1997.

CHAPTER 12

FRANK S. LUSK

BASKET OF DREAMS

O N A BROAD METAL shelf in the cavernous Collection Center of the Wyoming State Museum in Cheyenne stands a grand basket of willow and cottonwood. Its soft golden patina of perhaps a hundred years or more glows from age and use; geometric patterns twine over its surface. But unlike the vessel cited in the childhood tale, the boy Ali Baba does not hide there in fear of the forty thieves. Rather, within the coils of this *olla* we find the hand-woven history of the American Indian and the vision of pioneer Frank S. Lusk.

As the New York native recalled, his interest in Indian artifacts and his love of Wyoming started in 1877. He had a cattle business near Greeley, Colorado, and his family asked that he accompany the body of a friend back east to be buried. Because the dead man had once spent much time in Cheyenne, Frank honored his companion by visiting that "Magic City on the Plains." "Everyone was so nice," he wrote later, "that I was very much impressed with the class of people in the Territory." So two years later, he relocated his Node cattle ranch—named for his brand—to the Niobrara River near its source in Wyoming and began driving his livestock into the Hat Creek Basin country. During his life there, he also began acquiring a collection of rare Native American artifacts, including the aforementioned basket.

Frank bought some additional land in 1881, where the Black Hills stage road crossed the Niobrara, and the following year established a horse ranch on a site that would later become the city of Lusk, Wyoming.

The next six years, however, proved less successful. After an unsatisfactory cattle venture in the Bighorn Basin and two disastrous

Frank S. Lusk (April 27, 1857–August 6, 1930), rancher, railway director, coal mining executive, and banker, left a permanent legacy in Wyoming by founding three important communities there: Lusk and Glenrock in 1887 and Casper in 1888. (Stagecoach Museum, Lusk, Wyoming)

winters in 1885–87, he turned to more lucrative ventures: transportation, energy, and town-site development. When the Wyoming Central Railway organized in 1886, Frank was one of its directors. He was also vice president and general manager of the Shawnee Coal Company, which gave the Wyoming Central's parent company, Chicago & Northwestern Railroad, access to the coalfields in the high plains. During that time, Frank continued adding a wide variety of basketry, weapons, and related treasures to his Indian collection.

Because Lusk offered the only post office on the projected rail line into the Territory, it became the company's headquarters from which Frank developed other communities. He later said that when he rode horseback across the surrounding lands in January 1887, he found no ranches or towns between Fetterman and Lusk. So he initiated legal actions for securing rights to land along the Platte River and, the following July 8, he filed with Territorial authorities for the township of Douglas on behalf of the Wyoming Central Railway company. Also, thanks in part to his initiatives and the rail line's extension, Glenrock and Casper, respectively, came into being in 1887 and 1888. Frank subsequently took up contracting and superintended work on the railroad that once ran from Kansas City to Mexico City. And during 1902–04, his firm built the mountain section of the Moffat (Colorado) railroad before he moved to Montana and built the double tunnels there for the Northern Pacific and Milwaukee Railroad in the western part of that state. Leaving railroading in 1907, he moved to Missoula, Montana, where he made his home and became president of the city's First National Bank.

Although during his later years he gradually disposed of most of his properties in Wyoming, he "still retained the feeling that Wyoming...was really my home state." In appreciation for his love of that land as well as his good fortune and friends during the thirty years he lived there, he donated to the Wyoming State Museum his ethnological collection of more than 325 items representing at least twenty-four tribes of Native American peoples from the Plains, Desert Southwest, Northwest Coast, Alaska, and California.

On August 9, 1930, with his great basket of dreams filled—figuratively—to the brim, Frank died at age seventy-three in Missoula. Family subsequently interned his remains in Cleveland, Ohio.

✧ SOURCES CITED ✧ Several original sources proved invaluable to my research for this story. First was the letter that Frank Lusk wrote on February 4, 1924, while living in Missoula, Montana, to Mrs. Cyrus Beard in Cheyenne. That correspondence, which provides details about his life, may be read at the Wyoming State Archives. Second were the many important Indian artifacts from Lusk's personal collection now owned by the Wyoming State Museum. These

This granary basket, thirty-one inches high, stored a wide variety of crops for Apache Indians. Such containers served particularly well in the dry climate of the Southwest where they preserved dried corn, squash, beans, and other edible plants. The dark, vertical stairstep design is a devil's claw (Martynia), *a southwestern plant named for its talon-shaped seed pod.* (Wyoming State Museum)

include the magnificent Apache basket (artifact #21.1.271) and its accession files which trace some of its history.

The curious reader can learn more about Lusk's life in such published sources as *Progressive Men of Wyoming* (Chicago: A.W. Bowen & Co., 1903); "Frank Lusk Founded 3 Wyoming Towns," *Lusk* (Wyoming) *Herald*, May 24, 1956; and his obituary: "Wyoming Pioneer Dies at Missoula," *Wyoming State Tribune*, Cheyenne, August 13, 1930.

An appreciation of Lusk's superlative basketry collection can be gained from Otis Tufton Mason's *American Indian Basketry* (New York: Dover Publications, Inc., 1988) and the State of Wyoming Historical Department's *Quarterly Bulletin* (Vol. 1, Nos. 1 and 2), August 15, 1924.

This chapter first appeared, in a slightly different form, in the *Casper Star-Tribune*, July 17, 1996.

CHAPTER 13

Cheyenne Indians Baseball Team

Their Lives Were a Game

N<small>OT QUITE A CENTURY</small> ago, the mighty Cheyenne Indians flailed the hides of animals to help bring fame to themselves and satisfy their followers. But they beat not on bison skins, but on horsehide-covered spheres. And they were not indigenous natives of this land, but Anglo-Europeans who played and paid their way as a baseball team.

It's true. The national sport, brought to Cheyenne at least as early as the 1860s by an influx of military and settlers, slowly gained popularity as players with business, civic, professional, and athletic clubs refined and practiced their game. Not only did they play each other, but occasionally the "Cheyennes" formed an all-star team that traveled to nearby towns as well as to bordering Nebraska and Colorado to compete against rival clubs. The addendum "Indians" apparently evolved naturally rather than being bestowed by management or chosen by the players. It seems to have first appeared in print in a July 24, 1899, *Denver Post* sports story: "The Indians from Cheyenne came to Denver to play ball yesterday and after their first inning with the Denver team demonstrated to the fullest satisfaction of the audience that they were ball tossers *par excellence*."

Exactly eight months later, the "Magic City's" amateur sport became a commercial enterprise, when the Cheyenne Athletic Park Association (CAPA), administered by president Ed Vreeland and secretary-treasurer Ed Gerrans, filed articles of incorporation with the Wyoming Office of the Secretary of State. The company was capitalized at a thousand dollars, with two hundred shares each valued at five dollars. Vreeland and Gerrans sat on its board of trustees, as did George S. Walker, John Popp, and Maurice Dinneen, who also

The Cheyenne Indians' glory year was 1923: with twenty-eight wins and only one loss, the team earned the "Little World Series" championship in Denver. (Wyoming State Archives) managed the organization's baseball team. The players, according to the agreement, got "90 percent of the net receipts, after expenses are defrayed, the remaining ten percent going into the treasury of the association."

Prior to incorporating, the Indians played their games at Lakeside Park along the north shore of Minnehaha Lake. CAPA's officers subsequently obtained a three-year lease for land further north and "one block back of the Bradley houses near the cemetery." There, in mid-May 1900, they built a fenced-in ballpark and stadium with a 700-person capacity. On Sunday, May 3, only a few days after its completion, roughly three hundred spectators paid thirty-five cents each for a grandstand seat or a quarter for the bleachers, and watched their Indians win the season opener against the local Fort Russell Blues by a score of 22 to 30.

Apparently satisfied with their team's first professional performance, CAPA's trustees soon thereafter invested $125 in new uniforms: gray shirts emblazoned with "Cheyenne" in maroon letters, gray pants, and maroon caps and stockings.

Despite a sometimes-fickle public whose gate revenues might yield "less than one dollar a player," the Indians enjoyed more than a few highly successful seasons. Its glory year, in fact, came in 1923 when the team finished with twenty-eight wins and only one loss while winning the Little World Series championship in Denver. That season the Indians scored a total of 263 runs while their opponents could but muster a combined score of 77. And every regular player, with one exception, batted better than .300.

The next eighteen years, however, saw the once powerful Indians dwindle from professional Class A to semi-professional Class D status in 1941, when it played its last official game as part of the Western Baseball League. That latter organization succumbed the following February to manpower and economic pressures brought about by the advent of World War II.

❧ SOURCES CITED ❧ Although a careful study of several artifacts and their accession papers in the Wyoming State Museum—an autographed glove (artifact #86.5.3) and ball (#86.5.5)—provided some insight into the team and some of its members, most background information for this story came from secondary sources.

The following Cheyenne newspaper articles offer a quick review of the legendary nine. In the *Daily Leader:* "Town Talk," April 7, 1888. In the *Daily Sun-Leader:* Base Ball," August 7, 1899; "Five Errors Lose Game," July 24, 1899; and "A Brilliant Game," July 26, 1899. In the *Wyoming Tribune:* "Within Two Weeks," April 24, 1900; "Ball Game Today," April 29, 1900; "Base Ball Notes," May 8, 1900; and "The Lineup." Decades later, the *Daily Leader* commented on the team's demise in "Pickett Sees Little Hope for Western," February 25, 1942. Another fine story, "Home Runs on the High Plains," co-authored by Jim Beahn and Ann Nelson, appears in *Buffalo Bones IV: Stories from Wyoming's Past* (Cheyenne: Wyoming State Press—Wyoming State Archives, no date).

This chapter first appeared, in a slightly different form, in the *Casper Star-Tribune*, July 28, 1996.

CHAPTER 14

Chinese Miners

THERE'S NO GOOD TIME FOR A TERRIBLE TALE

*A*LONG THE ROCKY sagebrush slopes of southwestern Wyoming in 1864, a grime-encrusted town burst like a boil through the sandy soil near a fount that inspired its name: Rock Springs. The town's rapid growth stemmed not from its role as a stage stop, nor from the westward expansion of people representing many nationalities. Rather, pioneers flocked there to dig coal from rich, ebony veins that lay deep beneath the tents and shacks they hastily erected.

But nine years after its first settlers arrived, big troubles found them. The Union Pacific Coal Company's management cut its production costs in 1873 by shaving miners' pay from a nickel to four cents per bushel while adding twenty-five percent more work hours. When angry Anglo-European laborers in Rock Springs and at nearby Carbon staged a walkout, the firm countered by hiring Chinese strikebreakers. Fearing violence and the destruction of railway property, the company's leaders requested the help of Wyoming's Territorial Governor John Thayer. He responded by urging the federal government to send its troops to the troubled spot. The timely arrival of the United States military helped prevent the insurrectionists from firing more than one errant shot in anger.

During the next ten years, the Union Pacific's management continued importing Chinese workers to dig and process the fossil fuel that powered locomotives and steam engines until such workers outnumbered white miners by nearly two to one.

Finally, at about six o'clock the morning of September 2, 1885, resentment over wages and competition for work erupted when a contingent of white miners startled Chinese workers by stoning them as they exited Mine No. 6. Six hours later, another contingent of seventy miners charged from saloons, joined with an equal number of local white men, and stormed the nearby Chinese settlement. In the melee that followed, thirty Chinese died violently, including two who burned to death in their homes. Fourteen more were severely injured. When about 550 Chinese then ran panic-stricken into the surrounding hills, wolves killed two more. Twenty-six of them fled twelve miles west to the Green River and disappeared. Only a few of their possessions, such as some pottery and a few shards of glass, survived the fires that spread and destroyed their tinder-dry shacks. Property losses amounted to about $140,000.

Governor Francis E. Warren, who later became a United States senator, departed Cheyenne immediately for the troubled zone. He also wired Washington, D.C., requesting help. Several days later President Grover Cleveland ordered federal troops to the scene to protect the populace. Upon receipt of that directive, 250 soldiers left Evanston and escorted the surviving Chinese back to Rock Springs on September 9, exactly one week after the troubles there.

Although authorities subsequently accused sixteen persons with a host of crimes against the Chinese, the Sweetwater County grand jury refused to hand down indictments and the guilty were never brought to justice.

❧ SOURCES CITED ❧ I thought I knew much about the infamous Chinese Massacre near Rock Springs. But upon seeing at the Wyoming State Museum a soy-sauce jug (artifact #69.145.3) and ceramic jar (#69.145.5) that survived that horror, I realized that I not yet fully understood the human elements of that tragedy. Those artifacts impelled me to call for their accession papers so that I could learn how they came into the museum's possession and what they could tell me about the sad souls who lost their lives that day.

I found helpful historical context in *History of Wyoming* (Lincoln, NE: University of Nebraska Press, 1978), written by the Cowboy State's historian emeritus, T. A. Larson. Invaluable, too, was

At the Chinese Massacre in Rock Springs, Wyoming, twenty-eight resident Chinese lost their lives, including two who were burned to death in their homes. This painting by T. de Thulstoup appeared in Harper's Weekly, *September 26, 1885.* (Wyoming State Archives)

Henry F. Chadey's pamphlet *The Chinese Story & Rock Springs, WY* (Rock Springs, WY: Sweetwater County History Museum, no date).

Those curious about this scar on Wyoming's historic hide may find more details in Clayton D. Laurie's "Civil Disorder & the Military in Rock Springs, WY: The Army's Role in the 1885 Chinese Massacre," *Montana Magazine* (Vol, 40, No. 3), Summer 1990, and "John M. Murmann's 'War in the Mines,'" *In Wyoming* (Vol. IX, No. 2), June-July 1976.

This chapter first appeared, in a slightly different form, in the *Casper Star-Tribune*, September 1, 1996.

CHAPTER 15

MARTHA WELLNITZ

QUILTER LIVED IN WYOMING CAPITOL BASEMENT

THE GOLD-LEAFED DOME of her home gleamed brightly as the stout matron left the grey granite building and strode down the broad, paved walk. There at the corner of Twenty-fourth Street and Capitol Avenue, she left a small empty pail for Johnny Sloan's milk wagon service, then strode back to the neat but spare quarters that she shared with her family at Wyoming's most prestigious address: the State Capitol Building (see chapter 20: "More Than a Cup of History").

Born in August 1848, in DeKalb County, Missouri, young Martha Frances Snowden relocated with her family to Kanesville (later known as Council Bluffs), Iowa, and then to Omaha, Nebraska. Thirty years later, on the advice of a friend, she moved to Cheyenne and in 1880 purchased a small dressmaking shop at the southeast corner of Sixteenth and Pioneer Streets. Soon thereafter, at a First Baptist Church prayer meeting in the old Laramie County Courthouse, she met Elam Solomon Emerson whom she married on September 22, 1881. Two children, Paul H. and Grace S., were born to the couple before Elam died in 1885 from an injury incurred during athletic competition with fellow Union Pacific Railroad workers. To make ends meet "Mattie" took in roomers.

On May 2, 1891, Mattie married Julius Wellnitz, a Prussian German immigrant who worked at the local railroad coal chutes. With Mattie's encouragement, however, Julius got a job in September 1894, as a janitor at the State Capitol Building, and a year and a half later the family moved into a basement apartment there. While living in what the children referred to as their "grand house," the artistic woman kept busy with a wide variety of hand work: tatting,

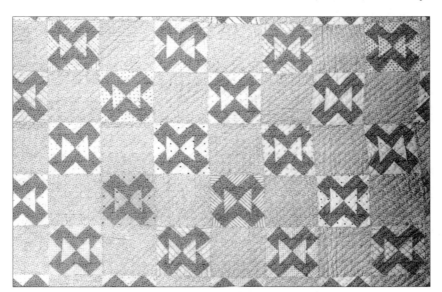

This "Double Z" or "Brown Goose" quilt measures 90 by 64 inches. It was pieced by Martha "Mattie" Frances Snowden Emerson Wellnitz around 1900 while she lived with her husband and children in a basement apartment in Wyoming's State Capitol. Its colors are predominantly yellow, black, white, and pink. The quilt's backing is a yellow, red, and black print fabric. (Wyoming State Museum)

crocheting, beadwork and, most of all, quilting. She also joined the Pioneer Club as a charter member and became socially active in the Eastern Star, the women's branch of the Masonic Lodge.

Despite their relative isolation in the State House, which until the town grew up around it was situated on the northern outskirts of town, the Wellnitzes met many of Wyoming's leaders. Ever resourceful, Mattie started serving luncheons to as many as eleven legislators at a sitting. In winter months, many preferred to dine at her table rather than brave the weather to reach the nearest restaurant eight blocks away. In this way, she helped finance her son's education at Harvard Medical School. Residence in the Capitol also influenced her daughter Grace's future. After obtaining state government employment, she worked her way up through the ranks and by 1931 achieved the position of deputy state auditor.

When Julius died in 1905, Mattie Wellnitz moved in to Grace's Cheyenne home and remained until she died there on August 26,

1931. Following funeral services at the local Baptist Church her family returned her body to Omaha for internment there.

✤ SOURCES CITED ✤ A glorious quilt exhibit at the Wyoming State Museum—and my wife's love of that art form—first brought Martha Wellnitz to my attention. Not only are the colors of her quilts like candy for the eyes, but her fine, neat stitches are impressive even to those not comparably crafts-inclined. So after seeing her handiwork and learning that she had lived in the Wyoming State Capitol, I examined the accession record (#64.10.394) for a piece that especially had caught my eye: a classic "Double Z" or "Brown Goose" pattern quilt.

To better understand that gifted lady who lived beneath the dome, I turned to those few articles that had recorded her life: "Death Claims Mrs. Martha Wellnitz," *Wyoming Eagle,* Cheyenne, August 26, 1931, and an untitled obituary in the August 28, 1931, *Wyoming Tribune.* And to learn more about the art that seemed to occupy most of Mattie Wellnitz's leisure hours, I also studied *Gatherings: American Quilt Heritage* (Paducah, KY: American Quilters' Society, 1995).

This chapter first appeared, in a slightly different form, in the *Casper Star-Tribune*, September 15, 1996.

CHAPTER 16

SEWELL NEWHOUSE

TIP YOUR TOPPER TO THE TRAPPERS

IN THE EARLY 1800s the top hat reigned supreme in the fashion world. In fact, most dapper dandies attending weddings, Sunday services, or fancy dress balls chose to wear "toppers" fashioned from the glossy, waterproof underfur of semiaquatic rodents of the genus Castor. Most of us best know those critters as beavers.

Perhaps more interesting to the student of history is that this curious vogue set forces and events in motion that helped open the American West. As the beaver supply dwindled in Europe and eastern North America, mountain men followed the sun into the then-unexplored lands of the Louisiana Purchase. For a few decades, until another fashion whim—the silk hat—sharply reduced the demand for the precious pelts in the 1840, trappers of many nations joined in the race for furs.

To harvest beaver, Indians and white trappers first chopped through winter's ice on beaver runs. Then they set snares and deadfalls, constructed so that a gate, log, or other weight would fall on the water-loving creatures. Later they returned to retrieve their prey and reset their traps.

Exactly when the first steel traps appeared in America is not clearly recorded. Some speculate that settlers of France's first colonies in Nova Scotia and on the St. Lawrence River, during the first decade of the seventeenth century, used them to kill pests and catch small mammals and birds for food. Englishmen who settled along the Atlantic Coast in the early 1600s may have also used such traps.

What is known is that a forge in the central New York village of Oneida Castle sired the American trap industry that was born in

The No. 4 double long-spring beaver trap was invented by Sewell Newhouse and patented on September 26, 1911. According to an imprint on the inner band, the beaver-hide top hat was "Made in Paris." (Wyoming State Museum)

1823. Sewell Newhouse, the seventeen-year-old son of a blacksmith, used his father's shop and its equipment to turn out guns and traps for his own use. He used metal scraps from his forge to form the bottoms and crosspieces of his snares. Then, from old ax blades, files, and worn-out scythes, he fashioned the springs that triggered his traps.

Sometime prior to 1848, Sewell Newhouse and his family joined the Oneida Community, a communistic society of "Perfectionists," at a time when the group lived on its own industry. Men, women, and children of the group rallied to help manufacture the traps. So effective were those snares that they became the envy of their neighbors, to whom Newhouse and his brethren sold them for sixty-two cents apiece. In fact, the increase in sales soon forced Newhouse to invent special equipment to handle the growing work load so that within a decade after his arrival in Oneida, machines made most of his traps. As authority Carl P. Russell noted in his book *Firearms, Traps & Tools of the Mountain Men,* "The best grade of traps made by the Oneida Community retained the trade name 'Newhouse' for more than a hundred years."

Although the firm's name evolved as mergers and growth changed its mission, the company remained in continuous operation for more than seventy-two years. In the 1920s, with its flatware and silver businesses prospering, Oneida sold its trapping enterprises.

❧ SOURCES CITED ❧ The accession records at the Wyoming State Museum for a beaver trap (artifact #67.160.13) and top hat (#81.1.94) unquestionably will enlighten a serious student of this subject. But to put such information in perspective, I recommend these secondary sources: Carl P. Russell's *Firearms, Traps & Tools of the Mountain Men* (Albuquerque, NM: University of New Mexico Press, 1967); "Minnesota Historical Society Collects Animal Traps," *Minnesota History*, Winter 1972; and Mary Belle Grant's "Colorado's Busy Builders," *Denver Post*, February 18, 1968.

This chapter first appeared, in a slightly different form, in the *Casper Star-Tribune*, October 27, 1996.

CHAPTER 17

SHOSHONE CHIEF WASHAKIE

DEER-HIDE DRAMA DEPICTS DARING DEEDS

A MIRROR HAS TWO faces: the image caught on glass and that perceived by the one who sees it. The same may be said of history. Consider the life of Chief Washakie, who led the Shoshone Indian tribe for sixty years (1840–1900). Most written accounts of his life focus on his lineage, his friendship with the white man, his dignity, bravery, bearing, and longevity. Washakie and his sons, however, recorded the chief's blood-spilling deeds rather than his bloodlines, and they did it well with pictographs on at least nine animal hides and panels painted on military target canvas.

Washakie's son Charles created one such painting on tanned deerskin in 1931 while he lived on Wyoming's Wind River Reservation. The pictographs describe the episodes as follows:

Scene 1 (top row, left): Washakie shoots a Blackfoot in an Owl Creek Mountains cave.

Scene 2 (top row, center): A Sioux shoots his rifle at Washakie during their running battle.

Scene 3 (top row, right: A mounted Washakie strikes a Sioux with his rifle butt.

Scene 4 (second row, left): Afoot with rifle and shield, Washakie leads his horse as he attacks a Cheyenne armed with a bow and arrows.

Scene 5 (second row, left of center): Washakie, on a black horse, encounters a Crow believed to be Chief Big Robber. Their war of words sparked the July 2, 1866, battle of Crowheart Butte, where Washakie allegedly killed his enemy and ate his heart.

This tanned deer hide was painted in 1931 by Charles Washakie to depict some of the favorite exploits of his famous father, Chief Washakie. (Wyoming State Museum)

Scene 6 (second row, right of center): Washakie, with a hide over his left arm and a rifle, battles an armed warrior wearing a war bonnet.

Scene 7 (second row, right): A Crow, who appears to hold some medicine items, is killed by the mounted Washakie in the vicinity of present-day Cody, Wyoming.

Scene 8 (third row, left): The meaning of the three tipis is not known.

Scene 9 (third row, left of center): Washakie, standing with an upraised sword and rifle, kills a fallen brave with his own blade.

Scene 10 (third row, center): Bonneted with eagle feathers, Chief Washakie holds a pipe.

Scene 11 (third row, right): Although Washakie fought many battles, he suffers his only known war wound—an arrow in his cheek—during this fight with five Blackfeet near Sage Creek.

Scene 12 (bottom row, center): Washakie skins a dead bison.

Scene 13 (bottom row, right): Washakie, on horseback, shoots his arrows at a wounded, fleeing bison.

Fortunately, what Charles's bright paints failed to capture about his father's life, historians have preserved in print. Washakie, which means "Killing (While) Running," found life around 1798 as Penna Gunna ("Sweet Smell"), the son of a Flathead father and a Shoshone mother. It is believed that he took his latter name—a tribute to his prowess as a hunter and warrior—around 1843 after he returned to his mother's tribe and rallied his own band of Shoshones in the Green River Basin during a time of tribal anarchy. Roughly seven years later, his people accepted him as their chief, a position he served with distinction. In fact, thanks to his exemplary leadership of the Shoshone and his friendship for the white man, the United States government honored him by renaming Camp Brown (originally called Camp Augur) in 1878 as Fort Washakie. The military had first built that installation near Wyoming's Wind River Range at Washakie's request for the protection of his people. When President Ulysses S. Grant subsequently presented him with a silver-trimmed saddle in Washington, D.C., the chief responded by saying, "Do a kindness to a white man; he feels it in his head, and his tongue speaks. Do a kindness to an Indian; he feels it in his heart; the heart has no tongue."

But his heart gave out at the age of 102 years and he died at home on February 21, 1900. Two days later, officers and men of the First United States Cavalry buried him with full military honors in the military cemetery named in his honor at Fort Washakie.

⚭ SOURCES CITED ⚭ Without question, the most important primary source regarding Chief Washakie's distinguished life must be the deer-hide painting that he and his son made to illustrate his exploits. It and the accession records (#86.6.1) that tell of its history may be seen at the Wyoming State Archives.

Chief Washakie, who led the Shoshone Indian tribe for sixty years, won the hearts of his people and the praise and admiration of such whites as President Ulysses S. Grant. (Wyoming State Archives)

Nearly as important as the accession records is a secondary source also held by the museum: James J. Stewart's *Historic Shoshone Elk Hides Depicting Chief Washakie's Warrior Exploits* (publisher not identified, 1991). I recommend, too, the study of the "Chief Washakie" vertical subject file at the Wyoming State Archives; it contains the following excellent articles about him and his family: "Life Sketch of Chief Washakie, Shoshone Chief" (source and date not shown); "The Redskin Who Saved the White Men's Lives" (reprint from 1961 *American Heritage* magazine), *Denver Post Empire Magazine*, August 13, 1961; Jeff Clack's "69 Years Ago - Great Chief Washakie Dies," (source and date not shown), "Wm. L. Simpson," *Big Horn Hot Springs Health Reporter*, Thermopolis, WY, April 1927, and Mae Urbanek's *Wyoming Place Names* (Missoula, MT: Mountain Press Publishing Company, 1988), pp. 31, 74.

This chapter first appeared, in a slightly different form, in the *Casper Star-Tribune*, November 10, 1996.

CHAPTER 18

John C. Coble

SHOOTIN' THE BULL IN THE OLD CHEYENNE CLUB

N O DOUBT ABOUT it. The bull and the cow were ugly critters. At least John Coble, Jr., thought that to be true when he saw them Saturday afternoon, September 14, 1895, in downtown Cheyenne, Wyoming. In a drunken rage, Coble pulled his pistol and twice shot the cow's left front leg.

That reckless act caused quite a stir. You see, the bovine he shot was featured on a prized piece of artwork that decorated a paneled wall of the famed Cheyenne Club's bar.

The next day the Club's president, William Sturgis, Jr., convened a special meeting of his board to introduce the following resolution:

> *Whereas, charges of a serious nature have been made by the House Committee against John C. Coble to the effect that his conduct in the Club House... while drunk was such as to call for his expulsion from the Club.*

Unwilling to pass judgment without first giving Coble a chance to defend himself, the officers barred the accused "from the use and privileges of the Club," pending an in-person explanation. Two weeks after his barroom spree, the contrite Coble stood before his accusers on September 28 and not only apologized for his behavior, but offered to repair, as much as possible, any damages done. Although he suffered only a reprimand, Coble still contended the painting was "a travesty on purebred stock" and later resigned his membership in the prestigious organization.

It is unlikely that John Coble, Sr. would have anticipated, much less approved, such conduct in his son's future when his wife, Hettie

John C. Coble, pioneer Wyoming cattle baron, added infamy to his resume with his employment and defense of Tom Horn, the feared stock detective. (Wyoming State Archives)

(Williams), gave birth to junior on June 4, 1858, in Carlisle, Pennsylvania. Following an elementary public school education, young John went to Pittsburgh where he attended Chambersburg Academy as well as Duffs College. Still later, he enrolled in Dickinson College at Carlisle. After graduating with the class of '76, he moved to Nebraska where, the following year, he launched his ranching career by collecting a herd of cattle which he grazed through the lush North Platte Valley. Before long, however, he went north to the Powder River country in Johnson County, Wyoming,

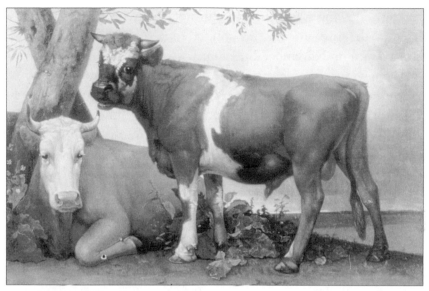

"The Young Bull" by Thomas Mesker is an 1885 copy of Dutch artist Paulus Potter's 1764 painting with the same title which hangs in the Hague Museum. Mesker honored the original by inscribing "Potter, 1764" on the left edge of the canvas above the reclining cow's shoulder. The two bullet holes in the cow's left front leg were made by John C. Coble's pistol attack. Former Wyoming Governor and then-U.S. Senator Francis E. Warren, together with rancher Thomas Sturgis, had purchased the painting on behalf of the Cheyenne Club during a trip to New York City in 1881. (Wyoming State Museum)

where he increased his assets by raising prize cattle and fine horses. As his business interests grew to include the prosperous Iron Mountain Ranch Company north of Cheyenne, he shifted his home base of operations in 1887 to adjacent Albany County where he wed Elsie Towson, a Laramie resident, and became active in the Masonic Lodge and the Benevolent and Protective Order of Elks.

Suspecting rustlers of looting their livestock, Coble and many of his friends hired the infamous Tom Horn and others of his ilk to protect their properties (see chapter 11: "Killing Men Was His Specialty"). Problems came to a head on July 18, 1901, when several shots from ambush killed Kels Nickell's fourteen-year-old son Willie near their property line in what is now Platte County. Soon thereafter, lawmen captured their prime suspect, the feared and despised

Horn. Following a lengthy trial during which Coble financed his friend's defense, authorities convicted the stock detective and hanged him on November 20, 1903.

Following Horn's death, Coble moved to Pinedale, Wyoming, where he continued his stock raising business. When his finances failed, however, he went via Texas to Nevada in June 1914. Shortly after his arrival in Elko, the despondent and nearly destitute Coble wrote to Wyoming rancher Frank Bosler requesting a job and threatening suicide if his former business associate denied him aid. That sad plea apparently fell on deaf ears, however, because Coble ended his life—only twenty-one days before Christmas—in the lobby of Elko's Commercial Hotel by firing a pistol into the roof of his mouth.

✤ SOURCES CITED ✤ The Wyoming State Museum files that accompany the "Young Bull" painting (artifact #A45.10.1), which once hung in the old Cheyenne Club, helped to tell much of this story. So, too, did a wide variety of materials in the "Cheyenne Club" vertical/subject file at the Wyoming State Archives: articles such as Dazee M. Bristol's undated and unpublished "The Cheyenne Club: Haven for the Luxury Loving Aristocrats of the Cattle Baron Days" and Cheyenne Chamber of Commerce Secretary Robert D. Hanesworth's letter to Mary McGrath, Wyoming State Historian, Cheyenne, June 15, 1945.

For a study of Coble himself, those interested should read his biography in *Progressive Men of Wyoming* (Chicago: A.W. Bowen & Co., 1903) as well as his obituary, "John Coble, A Suicide; Aided Famous Horn," *Cheyenne State Leader*, December 5, 1914.

This chapter first appeared, in a slightly different form, in the *Casper Star-Tribune*, January 19, 1997.

CHAPTER 19

Grace Raymond Hebard

A SOURCE AND SUBJECT OF WYOMING HISTORY

T HE GENTLEMAN BARELY heard Grace Raymond Hebard's soft, shallow breath as he sat in grim vigil by her bed. Called from his home in Oregon to Laramie, Wyoming, Lockwood Hebard knew that his sister's days—hours, in fact—were numbered.

Those who knew and loved the slim, starched lady who had seemed to march when she walked were saddened by her condition. However, they had expected it for some time. For more than two years, in fact, cancer had gnawed the woman's strength and vitality. But given her insatiable curiosity and sense of adventure, the seventy-five-year-old may well have felt in those last few lucid moments a sense of exhilaration, anticipating her reunion with her deceased parents, her sister Alice, her brother Fred, and her beloved housemate Agnes M. Wergeland. Even more exciting may have been the prospect of finally meeting those pioneers and heroes to whom she had dedicated the last fifty years of her life.

Grace was born in Clinton, Iowa, on July 2, 1861, as the third of four children of Congregational missionary parents who had moved west from New York state three years earlier. Because of poor health, Grace did not regularly attend public school. Her mother Margaret's home teaching, however, more than made up for that deficiency. So well did Grace learn those lessons that she went on in June 1882 to become the first woman to earn a Bachelor of Science degree in civil engineering from the State University of Iowa. (Later she would earn two more academic degrees, including a Ph.D. from Illinois Wesleyan University, and a host of other educational honors.)

Grace Raymond Hebard was an engineer, scholar, teacher, suffragist, attorney, champion athlete—a woman for all seasons. But her interest in preserving and marking Wyoming's historic sites once impelled her to described herself simply as a "humble follower of recording the records of the past." (Wyoming State Archives)

Following the death of her father later that year, Grace Hebard moved with her sister and mother to Cheyenne. There she found work as a draftsman in the United States Surveyor General's Land Office—the only woman in an organization of forty men. Her initiative and ability to make quality maps from raw field notes were rewarded nine years later with her promotion to deputy state engineer. In 1889 she also took on such extracurricular tasks as helping to draw up the petition for the Constitutional Convention of Wyoming's adoption of the women's suffrage amendment. Through such work and related political activities, she cultivated influential support which led to her appointment by Governor Amos W. Barber to the University of Wyoming's board of trustees.

So well did she adjust to her new responsibilities during her next seven years in Laramie that in 1898 she became the first woman attorney admitted to the Wyoming Bar. Also, according to Hebard, some members of the university's board of trustees offered her the position of president of that institution. She deferred, however, for what she claimed to be "good sound financial reasons."

But despite her obviously intensive scholarly pursuits, she found time for more leisurely activities. In 1900 she carded sixty-nine strokes for six holes of golf at a course in Laramie, becoming the first woman to win the Wyoming state championship for that sport.

She also began teaching political science and economics at the university and within three years became head of her department. Four years later, she became the first of her sex licensed to practice before the Wyoming Supreme Court. University of Wyoming officials also appointed her the institution's first librarian, a position she held until 1919. With newly expanded authority, she subsequently helped form the state's first library association, to which its members elected her as their first president.

Despite—or perhaps because of—her academic prowess and many contributions to higher education, Grace Hebard's growing power threatened some trustees and faculty members. Although personalities and petty politics seem to have spawned the dispute, her once strong base of support had so eroded by 1907 that a scandal erupted in which university powers scolded her for being "overbearing, galling and overly influential." They also formally accused her of slandering a fellow faculty member and his spouse. Some even sniped that her doctoral degree was "a pure fake."

In the wake of that rancor, she resigned from the board. At the suggestion of Dr. Agnes M. Wergeland, head of the university's history department as well as her companion, Hebard plunged instead into what would become a lifelong study of the Old West and began to teach that subject the following year. Her new vocation got a boost in 1915 with a summer tour of Wyoming, which Dr. Wergeland had planned before her death the year before The trip spurred her interest in preserving and marking sites of historical significance. The dedication of monuments, in turn, led her to research and extol subjects who became the protagonists of her later

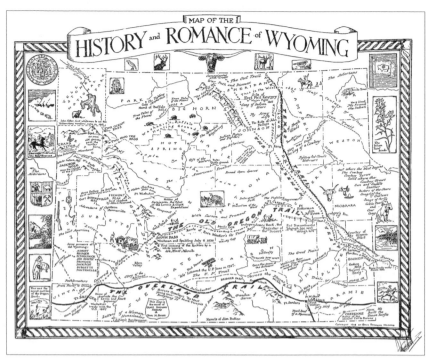

The "History and Romance of Wyoming" map, which marks many historic sites with the titles of books featuring state lore, was produced in 1928 by Grace Raymond Hebard and Paul M. Paint, an associate. (Wyoming State Archives)

historical studies. *The Pathfinders from River to Ocean*, published in 1911, celebrated the lives and times of many of those who tamed the frontier. Encouraged by the sale of that book, Hebard collaborated with the celebrated western historian E.A. Brinstool to tell the two-volume tale of miners and settlers who trod *The Bozeman Trail*. Then she plunged into her third major literary venture, a eulogy of the great Shoshone chief *Washakie*, which went to print in 1930.

But the subject with whom Hebard perhaps is most identified is the heroine of her most famous book, *Sacajawea*, first published in 1933. The Shoshone girl, who in 1805–06 led explorers Lewis and Clark across the northwestern part of the newly acquired territory, came to Hebard's attention when lecturers at the 1904 Exposition in St. Louis questioned the Indian guide's background and fate. Two years later, when a commission investigated the claim of Sacajawea's burial in Wyoming, Hebard felt stirred to prove that point.

Although her stories gained mass popularity, more than a few scholars have been less than enthusiastic about what they perceive to be her deductive approach to research. Their complaints stem in strong measure from her insistence that Sacajawea is buried in Wyoming, contrary to conflicting evidence offered by such formally educated and trained historians as the late T.A. Larson. Due to her training as a surveyor, one critic suggested she tended to fix, transit-like, on an idea, then pursue a single but rather general path of reasoning and body of evidence to substantiate her thesis. Although undoubtedly disappointed with such commentary, Hebard demurred that she simply considered herself a "humble follower of recording the records of the past." And even her antagonists concede that, despite their differences with Hebard, her preservation of historic documents and her recording of pioneers' eyewitness anecdotes are a great contribution to the history of Wyoming and the West.

But not even she, who embraced the study of time, could stop its progress. On Sunday, October 11, 1936, as the black hands of the clock touched 9:15 P.M., Grace Raymond Hebard joined those pathfinders about whom she had written and to whom she had dedicated so much of her time and talents.

❧ SOURCES CITED ❧ The serious student of Grace Raymond Hebard's work will find it thrilling to visit the Wyoming State Museum and examine her original "History & Romance Map of Wyoming" (artifact #93.14) and its accompanying accession records.

To learn about Dr. Hebard's life, a rapid review may be had by reading Janell M. Wenzel's superb thesis, *Dr. Grace Raymond Hebard as Western Historian* (Laramie, WY: University of Wyoming, 1960), Cora M. Beach's *Women of Wyoming* (Casper, WY: S.E. Boyer Co., 1927), Eva Floy Wheeler's *A History of Wyoming Writers* (privately published, 1981), and "In Memoriam: Grace Raymond Hebard, 1861-1936," a special University of Wyoming commemorative program, June 1937.

This chapter first appeared, in a slightly different form, in the *Casper Star-Tribune*, December 8, 1996.

CHAPTER 20

JOHN A. FEICK

MORE THAN A CUP OF HISTORY

Feby 2, 1887 - Dearest Wife! I just arrived at Cheyenne right side up and handled with care ... it was a long ride. I thought that I went around the world five times, can not tell you any thing about Cheyenne yet, just came in and is very dark ....

—John A. Feick after traveling from Sandusky, Ohio

TWO DECADES BEFORE John Feick arrived in Cheyenne, President Andrew Johnson signed the act creating Wyoming Territory on July 25, 1868. However, the territorial government did not organize until the following year when its officials designated Cheyenne as the capital. Because the new bureaucrats had no offices, they rented two rooms—one on Sixteenth Street and one on Seventeenth—in which they conducted business for roughly seventeen years.

Finally in 1886, Governor Francis E. Warren advised the legislature, "It would afford greater convenience to the public if the various territorial offices could be brought together in a central location." The congressmen agreed and authorized a structure to be built at a cost not to exceed $150,000.

You can not imagine what kind of a country this is you can go just one hundred miles straight out in the country and not see a house or a living sole, but wolves, prairie Dogs, Deer ... some very heigh mountains ....

To begin planning for construction, Warren appointed a five-man Capitol Building Commission chaired by Erasmus Nagle, a prominent Cheyenne businessman. Commission members selected two blocks on Hill Street, now known as Capitol Avenue, for the site. Soon thereafter they chose architect David W. Gibbs of Toledo,

The Wyoming State Capitol's design was done by architect David W. Gibbs of Toledo, Ohio. The A. (Adam) Feick & Bros. firm from Sandusky, Ohio, was to build the original structure of "wood... with an iron tower." (Wyoming State Archives)

Ohio, to design Wyoming's capitol "of wood construction with an iron tower," and the A. [Adam] Feick & Bros. firm of Sandusky, Ohio, to build it. To supervise the project whose final price tag would be $131,275.13, Adam Feick sent his twenty-four year-old son John to Cheyenne. During his fourteen months there John wrote to his wife not only about the project, but about life in Cheyenne, perhaps to reassure her that the frontier city was indeed civilized—to some degree.

> *This morning when I went to Breakfast I saw a Chinaman laying in the Street with his head cut off and it looked terrible ... You don't see as many drunkards in Cheyenne as you do in Sandusky and the town is kept very orderly....*

After subcontracting was gained with the Robert C. Greenlee Firm of Denver, groundbreaking took place on September 9, 1886. The Capitol's superstructure, featuring stone from a quarry in Rawl-

A commemorative china cup depicting the expanded Wyoming State Capitol was "Made in Austria [Vienna] for E.S. Johnson, Cheyenne, Wyo." Ephraim Johnson owned and operated the E.S. Johnson Grocery Company until his death in August 1930. Although the exact date of the cup's manufacture is not recorded, the lack of gold or yellow paint on the image's dome—the Capitol's most striking exterior feature—suggests the sketch was made between April 1890 (after the wings were added) and 1900, when the dome was gilded for the first time. (Wyoming State Museum)

ins, Wyoming, and a French Renaissance style of architecture, proceeded so quickly that officials laid its cornerstone with celebration on May 18 the following year.

> *My Dear Lizzie:… We are having lots of snow and bad weather, we will all be finished to go home Saturday…. Yours John A*

But as soon as the Commission submitted its final report on March 31, 1888, the Territorial Legislative Assembly passed a bill adding east and west wings to expand the new building, which many Wyoming state legislators already deemed too small. Although then-Governor Thomas Moonlight vetoed the additional construction, both houses of the legislature overrode his action and the state's chief executive reluctantly appointed the second Capitol Building Commission. Favorable conditions and expeditious workmanship ensured both new wings were completed in time for Wyoming's statehood celebration on July 10, 1890.

The third Capitol Building Commission, appointed by Governor John B. Kendrick, planned the expansion and supervised the March 1917 completion of the grand chambers in which the State Senate and House of Representatives have since convened.

The French Renaissance styled, three-story, grey sandstone structure is reminiscent of our national capitol. And because it is typical of many capitol buildings of its period, Cheyenne artist and architect Frederic H. Porter said,

> *We must respect this style and manner of our houses of State and honor their creation and the people who built them. In this way can there always be an ever present and visible reminder of past glories —by the careful and respectful preservation of the public edifices which so adequately portray our times, our customs and our fashions!*

And so, even as it serves as the Cowboy State's seat of government, Wyoming's capitol is also preserved in such commemorative objects as the handsome china cup.

❧ SOURCES CITED ❧ For more information about the cup upon which the image of the capitol is captured, a first-hand peek at that (artifact #64.10.74) and its Wyoming State Museum accession records is a must. Those more interested in the story of the capitol itself and its construction should see the brochure, co-authored by Rick Ewig, Linda G. Rollins, and Betty Giffin, entitled *Wyoming Capitol Centennial* (Cheyenne: Wyoming State Press, 1987); Frederic H. Porter's remarks are also found there. Another excellent source is Ewig's "Behind the Capitol Scenes," *Annals of Wyoming* (Vol. 59, No. 1), Spring 1987.

This chapter first appeared, in a slightly different form, in the *Casper Star-Tribune*, November 24, 1996.

CHAPTER 21

JOSEPH ELAM STIMSON

HE CAPTURED THE WEST WITH HIS CAMERA

THE WYOMING WIND whipped the dark, shroudlike cloth about Joseph Elam Stimson's head as he peered through his lens at the bare mound of muddy minerals in the foreground. His attention riveted on his subject, his fingers turned the knurled knob, moving the magnifier at the end of the leather bellows until the reversed and upside-down image sharpened on the ground glass focusing screen.

Suddenly a steaming spout of bright water boiled from the earth and shot high into the sky as it had regularly for perhaps a thousand years or more. But this time, with the geyser's mist alee of the breeze, Stimson snapped his shutter and trapped his subject's likeness inside his 8 x 10 format field camera. That 1907 scene of "Old Faithful" at Yellowstone National Park remained locked in the emulsion on the thin, glass plate negative until, with a bath of chemicals, the photographer freed the vista for the world to see.

Stimson was born May 18, 1870, on a farm near Brandy Station, Virginia, as the fourth boy of eight children. Their parents raised the family on farms in South Carolina and Nebraska. Two years after the death in 1884 of his physician father, sixteen-year-old Stimson traveled to Appleton, Wisconsin, where he apprenticed with a photographer-cousin to learn the art and chemistry of his craft.

In spring 1889, as the Wyoming Territory prepared to celebrate statehood the next year, Stimson moved to Cheyenne where he invested his savings in a small photo shop on one of the capital's dusty main streets. In that same city five years later, he met and married Anna Peterson and they subsequently had three daughters.

Joseph Stimson's view of Old Faithful in Yellowstone. (Wyoming State Archives)

Stimson's first glimpse into Wyoming's wild country came the year of his marriage when he processed pictures of the Big Horn Mountains taken by Elwood Mead, the state's first chief engineer. Awestruck by those visions of grandeur, Stimson joined Mead the following year for a return trip to northern Wyoming with their portable camera and a heavy black photographer's tent swaying precariously on the back of a pack horse. That trek proved to be the turning point of Stimson's photography career, which eventually spanned sixty-six years.

Union Pacific railroad executives, interested in attracting visitors to the areas they served, later hired him as an official photographer. From 1900 to 1910, Stimson traveled everywhere the U.P. rails

J.E. Stimson's vision, perhaps more than that of any other Wyoming photographer, caught and kept views of the state's early twentieth-century history that still are collected and cherished. (Wyoming State Archives)

could take him. Some of the communities whose pictures he snapped turned into cities; others faded to ghost towns. He also filmed scenes of industry and agriculture as well as many of our nation's pioneers. But his "grandscape" views of lakes, forests, and mountains drew the most public attention by winning awards at the 1903 Louisiana Purchase Exposition in St. Louis and at the Lewis and Clark Exposition the following year in Portland, Oregon.

Although the close of World War I ended Stimson's railway connection, his career took another upswing in 1929. His old friend

Mead, who had risen to the post of commissioner of the United States Bureau of Reclamation, hired the photographer to make a visual record of the Bureau's construction projects in the West. But only nine years later, Stimson went into semi-retirement when his beloved Anna died following a stroke.

Officials with the Wyoming Department of Commerce, however, encouraged him back to work in 1948 by hiring him to return to the Teton and Yellowstone country and film a series of scenes for their agency's files.

When Stimson died of a heart attack in Hartford, Connecticut, on February 8, 1952, he left a trove of more than 7,500 glass plate and nitrate negatives which his daughters sold to the Wyoming State Museum. Their father probably would have blessed their decision, because—in the words printed on the wrapper of each photo that left his shop—"It is given to few to create; to enjoy should be the inalienable birthright of all."

❧ SOURCES CITED ❧ To understand Joseph Elam Stimson, it should help to first study that which he seemed to hold so dear: his 8x10 field camera (artifact #52.40.2.a) that makes its home in the Wyoming State Museum. There you may also inspect the accession records that document the device's history and final journey to the site of some of the Cowboy State's finest historical artifacts.

For a one-stop read about Stimson's life, I can suggest no better book than Mark Junge's *J.E. Stimson, Photographer of the West* (Lincoln, NE: University of Nebraska Press, 1985). Several other fine secondary sources are Louise Stimson Hollowell's unpublished "Biography of Joseph Elam Stimson: Wyoming Scenes Photographer, 1889–1952," which is on file at the Wyoming State Archives, and two tributes: "Ex-Cheyenne Photographer Dies in Conn.," *Wyoming State Tribune*, Cheyenne, February 10, 1952, and "Final Rites Held for Former Cheyenne Artist," *Wyoming State Journal*, Cheyenne, August 17, 1953.

This chapter first appeared, in a slightly different form, in the *Casper Star-Tribune*, December 26, 1996.

CHAPTER 22

OWEN WISTER

WISTER WROTE THE WEST

The time: An evening, circa 1890
The place: Pennsylvania's posh Philadelphia Club
The characters: Two gentlemen, well bred and well groomed

*A*T A PROPERLY SET table, the two men enjoyed fine wine, dinner, and leisurely conversation. When their talk turned to America's western wilderness, one of them—a recent traveler there—is said to have asked, "Why isn't some Kipling saving the sage-brush for American literature, before the sage-brush and all that it signifies goes the way of the California forty-niner, goes the way of the Mississippi steamboat, goes the way of everything?"

Carried away by his own rhetoric, the speaker said to his companion, "I'm going to try it myself! I'm going to start this minute." Excusing himself, he went upstairs to the club library where he sat down, picked up a pencil, and began writing "Hank's Woman," his first tale about the West. *Harper's Weekly* bought the story on first sight and suggested to the thirty-one-year-old lawyer that he write some more.

Encouraged by that success, he soon gave up his law career and turned full time to writing, producing some of his finest work about the Wild West, including his 1896 short story collection *Red Men and White*, followed by *Lin McLean*, his first novel, and then *The Jimmyjohn Boss*.

He did not gain wide critical and popular success, however, until a few years later when the obscure short-story author suddenly became the most widely-read novelist on either side of the Atlantic. His name: Owen Wister. The novel: *The Virginian* (1902), a literary

Owen Wister, born near Philadelphia in 1860, was educated in Switzerland and England and later at Harvard. To ease his mental and physical health problems, he later visited Wyoming periodically. (American Heritage Center, University of Wyoming)

The handsome desk at which Wister wrote so many of his Western stories stands in the Owen Wister Room at the University of Wyoming's Coe Library. (American Heritage Center)

work credited by many for establishing the archetypal cowboy hero and villain who became prevalent in twentieth-century popular fiction and later, in movies, radio, and television.

Born July 14, 1860, in the Philadelphia suburb of Germantown, he was the son of Sarah Butler—whose mother was the famous English actress Fanny Kemble—and a prominent physician, Owen Jones Wister. After attending a host of boarding schools, including two in Switzerland and England, young Wister attended Harvard University (1878–82) from which he received an A.B. with honors in philosophy and English composition, as well as the highest honors in music. He then studied musical composition in Paris for a year and, having caught the favorable attention of composer Franz Liszt, seriously considered a career in music. His father soon squelched that dream, however, and urged him to take a job at Union Safe Deposit Vaults in Boston. But suffering increasing physical and emotional problems, Wister took his doctor's advice and, in June 1885, took the first of his many trips to Wyoming. There he found values and a lifestyle that appealed to his rugged individualism and great love of unspoiled nature.

Returning to Harvard that fall, he attended law school and four years later joined a Philadelphia law firm. His career there, however, proved short-lived. Following the August 1892 publication of "Hank's Woman," he turned his attention full time to writing about the new life he found in the West. Then—on April 25, 1897—Wister married his second cousin, Mary (Molly) Channing Wister; when she died in childbirth in 1913, she left him with six children.

In addition to his wonderful writings about the West, the prolific storyteller also wrote biographies about such celebrities as *Ulysses S. Grant* (1900) and (Theodore) *Roosevelt: The Story of a Friendship* (1930), and numerous nonfiction articles and essays for such popular periodicals as the *Atlantic Monthly, Harper's Weekly*, and the *Saturday Evening Post*.

Death penned *finis*, however, to the author's life on July 21, 1938, at North Kingstown, Rhode Island.

❧ SOURCES CITED ❧ Readers unfamiliar with Wister's work, or with but a passing interest in the West, may find their interest quickened after turning a few pages of the first-edition copy of his 1898 novel *Lin McLean* which may be read in the Owen Wister Western Writers Reading Room at the University of Wyoming's Coe Library.

Essential reading is the fine book edited by Fanny Kemble Wister, *Owen Wister Out West: His Journals & Letters* (Chicago: University of Chicago Press, 1958). For basic biographical information about the man, I suggest the following: James J. Martine, ed., *American Novelists, 1910-1945*, Vol. 9 (Detroit: Cole Research Co., 1981); Dennis Poupard, ed., *Twentieth Century Literary Criticism*, Vol. 21 (Detroit: Cole Research Co., 1986), and "Wister, Owen," *Colliers Encyclopedia*, (New York: Crowell Collier Publishing Co., 1963).

This chapter first appeared, in a slightly different form, in the *Casper Star-Tribune*, January 12, 1997.

CHAPTER 23

CHARLES E. MILLER

ICE AND WATER BROUGHT HIM DOWN

January 3, 1891. A trio of escaped criminals, their limbs poorly insulated with layers of clothing, walked by starlight through the winter waste toward the invisible line that divides Wyoming's high plain from that of Nebraska.

William Kingen, a one-time rancher, pointed the way, but ebony-skinned former United States Cavalry trooper Richard Johnson broke trail for the struggling cowman and their lean, sixteen-year-old companion Charley Miller. Night turned to day as Kingen's pinched hat plowed the sharp wind and sleet until his failing feet sometimes resisted even the most encouraging calls from his mates. Once brawny, Kingen tired easily now. He had two strikes against him: a recent undiagnosed illness and weakness due to fourteen months in jail for cattle rustling. Although Miller had spent much of his brief life riding shank's mare—making his way on foot—he, too, found himself losing interest in their trek.

Only the round-shouldered Johnson, with his comical, bewhiskered expression, wanted to continue. So he pleaded. He cajoled. The convicted moonshiner even tried unsuccessfully to carry the heavier Kingen on his bent back.

Hours later, as day faded for the third time since their terrible odyssey began, even Johnson's threats failed to motivate his comrades across the brittle, brown grass. Two hundred yards ahead of them, with the last rays of sun tap-dancing on the horizon, Johnson sat down and waited for his plodding partners. But now Kingen lurched to a halt. Charley, with numbed fingers and gunnysack-wrapped toes, also had come to the end of his trail. Their strength and wills flew south like birds as they slumped side by side into a small bison wallow. The warmth and weight of their bodies pressed slowly through the icy crust until the wiry grama grass, like an old mattress, bent to their shapes. Lying there, they tugged their coats tightly and pressed close to each other for protection against the wind's cruel teeth. Both immediately fell asleep.

Sympathizing with their plight, Johnson shuffled back over his faint tracks to where his fellow fugitives lay. But after waiting and suffering two more hours, he plunged alone into the waiting darkness. Johnson feared that if he stayed, death surely would find him on that God-forsaken plain.

❧

Who knows what last lucid thoughts crossed Charley's mind before sleep caught him —perhaps memories played in his dreams. Born to somewhat Spartan circumstances in New York City on November 21, 1874, Charley relied on siblings after their German mother died of consumption four years later. Their saloonkeeper father, also from *das Vaterland*, took his life the following year by ingesting Paris green, a poisonous compound usually used as an insecticide and pigment. In the wake of those tragedies, the Miller children were shuffled from home to home until 1881 when they entered New York City's Orphan Asylum. There they joined some two hundred other homeless and hapless youngsters.

On his twelfth birthday, asylum authorities found a home for Charley with a fruit farmer near Norfolk, Virginia. But that match failed. "I had a complaint while there," Charley later lamented, "and concluded the best thing I could do [was] to return and give the people no more trouble." When he returned briefly to the asylum, officials there gave him two new suits and shipped him west on an "orphan train" to Fillmore County, Minnesota. Upon arrival, he met his sponsor J.R. Booth and accompanied him back to his small spread near the village of Chatfield, about twenty miles southeast of Rochester. The arrangement seemed promising. The farmer even offered Charley an interest in the family's land if he

Hapless Charley Miller, whose life lasted only seventeen years, nine months, and a fistful of days, was the first and youngest person to be executed in the State of Wyoming as well as the first to be hanged there with a mechanized, water-driven, "no fault" trap. (Cheyenne Daily Leader)

worked faithfully. But Charley soon learned that "faithfully" meant plowing fields from the sun's first light 'til night. Fortunately, a sympathetic woman teacher shared Charley's dismay and forwarded his letters of complaint to the Children's Aid Society of New York. Touched by her compassion, the lad ran away from Booth and moved in with her family. He remained there until the farmer and one of his sons came for him a week later. After threatening "to tie him to a tree and cowhide him," they forced the truant into their buggy and returned to the farm. Soon thereafter, a passerby found

Charley at the edge of Booth's property and rescued him. All seemed well until the new custodian got drunk and drove him from the house and out of his life.

The following spring, in response to his grievances, Charley received a registered letter from the Children's Aid Society that included a five-dollar bill, a note from his sister, and instructions to pick up a railway ticket at the nearby Chatfield depot. Two days later he left for Leonardville, a small town twelve miles northwest of Manhattan, Kansas, where brothers Fred and Willie awaited him at the home of their guardian P.S. Loofbourrow, a postmaster and editor of the local *Monitor* newspaper. Loofbourrow soon found his new charge a home with Reverend J.H. Colt, manager of *The Enterprise*, a publication in nearby Randolph, Kansas. The boy learned the fundamentals of the printing trade there. Charley remained five months, counting on the preacher's promise of free board and clothes in exchange for his labors. But although the guardian fed and housed him, duds failed to materialize, so restless Charley packed his meager possessions into a valise pilfered from the minister and left in midwinter for the Omaha–Council Bluffs area. With no money, he begged food and hitched his way aboard the Chicago, Burlington & Quincy Railroad.

It is not known how he spent those frigid months, but in April 1889 "a commercial traveler" from Des Moines, Iowa, found the gaunt ragamuffin alone and forlorn in a depot at the western edge of that state. Upon learning about the boy's printing skills, the man took pity, escorted him to Glenwood, Iowa, and arranged for a home and job with Louis Robinson, editor of *The Opinion*. The newsman said:

> *We put him to work. Found a bright and a smart compositor. Our wife thought she saw a chance for missionary work, bought him a suit of new clothes, made him promise to go to church and Sunday school, had him bath [sic] and clean up, and he looked quite respectable. He went to Sunday school two Sundays and that ended it. He said Sunday school was too*

"pokey" and there was no fun there. He was fond of reading dime novels and had no taste for anything pure and good.

Although Charley acknowledged the Robinsons' fair treatment, the troubled youth said he so suffered "...with disease that I concluded I could stay with them no longer." The nature of his disease is unknown, but fourteen months later, light-fingered Charley pocketed $1.63 of Mrs. Robinson's change supply and again took flight, this time to Ohio via Chicago.

During the next year or so, the waif hitched rides on boats and trains throughout the northeast before looping back to the Midwest. Each day he fought a desperate battle against cold, hunger, the law, and, most especially, loneliness. But he most feared the threats of the boxcar toughs with whom he rode the rails. So with the last of the wages he had earned by washing dishes, he bought an old, nickel-plated .32-caliber revolver and five bullets for $1.25. With that new-found security, he also took a sobriquet. "Kansas Charley," he called himself. In true hobo style, he chalked his nickname on nearly every trackside water tank along his route. But with no money or job awaiting him in the Midwest, he was soon on the move again. This time he went west toward Wyoming which had joined the Union three months earlier as its forty-fourth state.

On the afternoon of September 26, 1890, at a stop just east of Sidney, Nebraska, Charley met two well-dressed young men from St. Joseph, Missouri, tramping on the train. Destined for Denver, Ross T. Fishbaugh—a grain company clerk and the sole support of his widowed mother—and his childhood companion, a saddler's son named Waldo B. Emerson, hoped for employment there. Although Charley had not shared their boxcar, the trio had arrived in Sidney aboard the same train at about noon. During that respite, Charley earned a paper-sack lunch from a baker by picking up loose coal near the tracks. A short time later he found Fishbaugh and Emerson sitting at the corner of Front Street and shared his food with them. The Missouri boys reciprocated by treating the lad in the shabby brown coat and threadbare pants to some beer at Sheriff

In Pine Bluffs, Wyoming, a bustling burg near the Nebraska border, Miller's victims ate their last meals. The town takes its name from the stubbed trees that beard the far ridge on the old Texas Trail. (Polly B. Burkett Collection)

Sam Fowler's saloon. While imbibing, Fishbaugh pulled a ten-dollar bill from his pocket and boasted, "That's the second one I busted today." That afternoon, the three young men tried boarding a freight, but brakemen caught them. Forced off the train west of town near the fairgrounds, the boys trudged back to Sidney with their belongings. At about nine-thirty that evening Charley noticed another freight crew preparing for departure. This time he climbed aboard an open livestock car, covered himself with hay, and fell asleep before the locomotive pulled out.

As the sun rose the next day, Charley awoke when the train shuddered to a stop near Nebraska's western border. Avoiding the trainmen's detection, he gingerly dropped to the ground with a load of hay in his arms and sneaked from boxcar to boxcar until he found one with a partly open door. As he tried to toss his grassy load inside, a voice called, "Hello, Kid." In the doorway above him, Fishbaugh's welcome hand pulled Charley up out of the wind and into the dark warmth of the car. A short time later the train crossed into Wyoming and stopped at Pine Bluffs, aptly named for the stubbed evergreens that crest those distinctive rocks along the Texas Trail. During that brief break, the trio ate breakfast in Mrs. Amanda Kaufman's hotel dining room.

Shortly after their meal the boys, soothed by full stomachs, returned to the shelter of the boxcar and removed their shoes, placing them neatly in the center of the floor. Emerson curled up on some railroad ties piled to within a foot of the roof at the west end of the car. Fishbaugh climbed up and fell asleep next to him, their heads resting on small pillows of loose hay. On an adjacent beam, a dark bottle gleamed with an inch or so of bronze-colored liquor. Some cold, crushed cigarette butts littered the spot where the boys had spat while they swapped lies. Minutes later the flagman's signal gave the "go" to the engineer, and the cars snapped together with loud clangs and clacks as the train slowly lurched west.

Mistaking Kingen's tremors for those of the train, Charley thought he still rode the boxcar. Instead, he found himself curled in the snow with his knees pulled tight to his chest. Twitching and shuddering, he nursed what little warmth remained in his small frame. "Johnson has shaken us, Charley," Kingen moaned; "Oh! I'm so worn out. I can go no further. Guess I shall die right here, but I would much prefer to die here than to go back to that jail in Cheyenne and die there." Although Kingen's broad body in its sturdy sack coat helped shelter the boy, both felons shivered uncontrollably. Hoping for some added protection against the harsh wind, Charley untied from his neck the empty flour sack in which he had carried their victuals, and pulled it over his head. The sack had already served as a scarf after they ate the last of their food. As the lad's breath warmed the inside of the stale bag, sleep once more took him into its arms.

Nestled peacefully among the rough-hewn oak logs being shipped from their home state, the Missouri boys slept in the car warmed by the high noon sun as the freight rumbled on towards Hillsdale, Wyoming. While they drowsed, Charley helped himself to the last of their whisky. Hoping for a morale boost from that last bit of "Dutch courage," he sucked the flask dry, but it only filled him with the chill of self-pity. "I felt homesick and cold," he said.

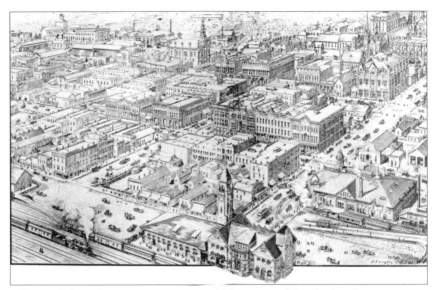

Cheyenne's busy downtown in 1890 might have seemed familiar to the sixteen-year-old former Gotham gamin Charley Miller even though Broadway's buildings in his native New York ranged from four to six stories at the time, while Cheyenne's were mostly two and three stories. (Wyoming State Archives)

"My clothes were ragged and I thought I was far from my brothers and all alone in the world, and I was hungry. My shirt was torn through at the elbows and my pants through the knees. I drank the whisky. I commenced feeling pretty good and felt dizzy. It made me pretty drunk."

In that stupor, Charley claimed later, he found a brief cure for his real and imagined ills. Furtively pulling the black-handled revolver from his hip pocket, the man-child crept to the side of the young men slumbering upon the ties. Then, raising its muzzle above his head, he ever…so…slowly…lowered it to within a few inches of Emerson's right temple. The explosion that followed instantly ended the nineteen-year-old traveler's life. Without missing a beat, Charley swung the barrel of his pistol toward the startled Fishbaugh's head. Again he fired point blank. Although mortally wounded, the twenty-one-year-old instinctively tried to stand, but his foot caught beneath a heavy log and he fell senselessly across an uneven pile of lumber near the door of the boxcar. With acrid smoke in his nose and the roar of gunshots ringing in his ears, Charley methodically searched his victims' pockets for valuables. From Emerson he stole two small case knives and a silver, open-faced pocket watch, but tossed aside its chain. Also, after finding a pistol in Emerson's pocket that was superior to his own, he squirreled that away, too, before tucking his own gun beneath the corpse. He robbed Fishbaugh's money, then dropped the empty purse on the floor. As the train churned toward its next stop, the dying man's blood pumped from the dark, open wound while moans oozed from his frothing lips.

> *It is not clear how much time elapsed, but Charley awoke to loud groans from his friend. "Oh, I'm so cold, Charley; so awful cold!" he mumbled through parched and bleeding lips. "Lay up close to me," said Charley. Kingen, his teeth chattering like a shaken sack of loose coins, pulled the youngster under the tent of his greatcoat. As the boy's face found the warmth of the rancher's armpit, Kingen's slow, failing heartbeat lulled the lad. Despite their pain, the weary pair again fell asleep.*

The waning clickity-clack of the wheels warned Charley that the train was approaching Hillsdale, a whistle stop nestled in a bare valley between treeless hills. Charley hopped out of the car. Finding his way to the section house, he asked John Brooks if he could spare some lunch. Never refusing a needy stranger, the powerhouse engineer offered his family's hospitality. During the meal, the boy told a confused, rambling tale of his travels. His destination? First he said Greeley, Colorado. The next moment he talked of Manhattan, Kansas. After eating his fill, Charley paid his host with two bits from his blood money before ambling back to the depot. Fearing he might be caught with the dead men's knives and gun, he cached them under a loose board at the west end of the platform.

In the meantime, as George Mannifee passed a boxcar during his routine check of the train, he heard strange sounds. Opening the door, the brakeman found an unconscious man with blood trickling from a wound in the right temple, the flesh still warm. As Mannifee's eyes adjusted to the darkness, he discovered a second young man. Like a traitor in his coffin, the body had lodged face down between some ties. Leaning closer, the railroader saw coagulated blood and a neat hole almost hidden by a large powder burn. A cheap, bright-skinned revolver with two empty shells in its chamber lay near the right side of the corpse. The startled Mannifee ran back along the tracks to the caboose and told associates of his discovery. When the brakeman led them back to the macabre scene, Fishbaugh's dull, harsh snore signaled his impending death. After making the victim as comfortable as possible, the trainmen wired news of the tragedy to authorities in Cheyenne.

As the freighter resumed its journey, Charley hoofed it to the Hillsdale depot and bought a ticket with a silver dollar before boarding a passenger train to Cheyenne.

When the freighter with its bloody cargo arrived in the capital at about two o'clock, officials unloaded the bodies into a wagon and sent them to the local drugstore. From there the corpse went to the undertaker at Warren's Emporium while the wounded man found a narrow cot at the Laramie County Hospital. Blood and black powder sponged from Fishbaugh's wan features revealed heavy eyelids and glazed orbs, harbingers of the young victim's certain fate. "Tall, strong, dark, lately shaven clean, [the patient] wore such clothes as a young man roughing it would choose from a fair wardrobe," reported a witness. As hospital staff removed the paralyzed man's clothes to search for other wounds, they found in his pockets a ring of keys, an express receipt for shipment of a valise to Denver, and a small, soft leather case of cards bearing his name. An envelope addressed to "Mr. Ross Fishbaugh, St. Joseph, Mo." contained letters of reference from two Missouri grain dealers praised the billing clerk's good habits and honesty. They lauded him, too, as "an exceedingly good judge of grain for a man of his age [who] writes an unusually good hand and is correct in figures and neat in all his work." Alas, despite his promising future, poor Fishbaugh died about four hours later without regaining consciousness.

In the meantime, Dr. Henry J. Maynard examined Emerson at the morgue. After concluding that a bullet in the brain caused the man's demise, the physician noted the youthful corpse's garments and general appearance: "…well clothed in a suit of fine fabric and good fit. He sported a new tie and had a natty fall overcoat. He was sandy complexioned, medium height and soft white hands."

That afternoon, the passenger train also arrived in Cheyenne carrying Charley with his ill-gotten funds. He heard men talking later in the streets about the Hillsdale murders, but he remained fearless. In fact, he celebrated his unexpected financial gain with a $1.65 shave and haircut with a spritz of tonic. He also bought a $2.25 shirt, polished off a two-bit meal with a dessert of doughnuts, and met Henry Bowland at Herman Kimme's Lakeside Saloon. Bowland, a handyman, befriended the boy and shared his bed there with him that night. The next morning, Charley hired on with some herders and helped them drive their sheep south to Grover, Colorado. Apparently overcome with guilt or fear of getting caught with stolen goods, he ditched Emerson's watch in a gopher hole. Three days later, when the flock arrived at its destination, Charley bought a Burlington train ticket to Concordia, Kansas, and from there he made his way back to his brothers' home in Leonardville.

As lawmen elsewhere spun theories and chased suspects, Laramie County Sheriff John A. Martin investigated the case in his own quiet way. Despite an early conclusion by a St. Joseph detective that a known, long-time enemy of the boys had murdered them, Martin proved that no such person had traveled into Wyoming with Fishbaugh and Emerson. Instead, witnesses described another youth thrown off the victims' train just west of Sidney. According to Martin, that same young man not only rode into Hillsdale on the dead men's freighter, but he also asked the fare to Manhattan, Kansas. With evidence gleaned from trainmen and other eyewitnesses at Pine Bluffs and Hillsdale, Martin shared the suspect's description with officials throughout the Rocky Mountains and Great Plains, most particularly with Sheriff Joseph M. Meyers of Riley County, Kansas.

❧

As October 12 dawned, Charley sat with a newspaper in the privy near Loofbourrow's Leonardville farmhouse. As he read, a story about his own crime caught his eye. Quickly leaving the out-house, he called brother Fred from the cabin and told him, "I was the boy who murdered Emerson and Fishbaugh." He did it, he said, for their money: "I was penniless, hungry and desperate." As the boys slowly realized the magnitude of those vicious acts, they cried so loudly that old man Loofbourrow responded to the noise. Upon learning the terrible truth, the newspaperman and his ward encour-aged Charley's surrender. Three days later he turned himself in to the startled Riley County sheriff at nearby Manhattan. Sheriff Mey-ers locked him up and wired his counterpart in Cheyenne that the killer of the St. Joe boys had confessed his crimes. Martin boarded a train and rushed to Kansas with a requisition, took Charley into custody and, with hardly more than a meal and a few hours' rest, Martin and his prisoner boarded a return passenger car to Wyoming on October 17. A curious crowd of two thousand greeted them in Cheyenne the following afternoon.

The next month, district court officials assigned the firm of Armstrong, Breckons & Taggart to defend the boy against the felony charges. Frank D. Taggart drew the proverbial short straw and became Charley's principal defense attorney. On November 10 a grand jury met and found the suspect guilty of four counts of murder: two pertained to Emerson and two to Fishbaugh. Upon his arraignment fifteen days later, the accused killer decided upon advice of counsel to plead not guilty to all charges.

The trial for his life began on December 7 when Charley, weak and pale from imprisonment, appeared in the Cheyenne court-house. Upon discovering the crowd assembled in the room, he seemed stunned by the attention, but quickly regained his compo-sure. Some of the spectators also may have also registered shock as they strained for each word of evidence, because for the first time in a Wyoming capital punishment legal case—and perhaps in any criminal trial in the state—both the defense and the prosecution cited *masturbation* in their respective cases. Attorney Taggart's wit-nesses asserted that, because Charley abused himself so habitually since the age of nine—"sometimes 3 or 4 times a day"—he lacked

Laramie County's red-brick courthouse was completed in January 1873. The County Jail and sheriff's residence can be seen just beyond the main structure. (Wyoming State Archives)

the energy, vitality, and, in fact, emotion needed for committing such a heinous crime. According to defense witness Dr. W.W. Crook, "The general effect of this act is to affect the nervous sensibility, the nervous power; the tendency is to reduce the nervous force, to lessen mental activity...to impair the brain power, a general disposition to reduce the forces of life...."

Laramie County attorney and prosecutor Walter R. Stoll countered through his own witnesses that Miller's psychosis and chronic self-abuse evidenced a perverse and criminal mind. But when challenged as to whether excessive masturbation produces homicidal mania, even Dr. W.A. Wyman, the prosecutor's key medical authority, acknowledged, "I don't think it can."

At least a score of spectators stood and craned their necks for prurient peeks at the defendant. Some of those witnesses to his testimony claimed that with his limp lips and sallow complexion, he looked immature and undeveloped. According to one, "His hair is light and thick and almost covers the forehead. His most prominent feature is his nose...large, somewhat hooked, and very thin." Four days later—December 11—the judge sent the jurors from the room. Incredibly, after deliberating only fifteen minutes, they returned to the court. All eyes in the room, except for those of the hushed officials, turned and fixed on Charley's face as the foreman pronounced the verdict: "Guilty of murder in the first degree."

The sun's frosted halo glowed through the noontime sky as Miller awoke to the stare of Kingen's glazed, bloodshot right eye. That sight so mesmerized him that he was slow to notice that the cowman's slack left lid nearly hid a dark-hued iris. Gradually Charley, mentally and physically numbed by cold, realized his friend's deep-purple skin proclaimed that death had arrived. Cracked lips, the lower one swollen and droopy, framed dull teeth. Long, shaggy, sandy-colored hair and a three weeks' beard accentuated the dead man's pinched and ghastly gaze. Those whiskers! They reminded Charley of some-thing... someone. He tried to remember who?... what?... Was it a former fellow prisoner, a relative, or was it simply Death in a bushy disguise, trying to lure him to a never-ending sleep?

The sun rays of December 1891's last day cast long, lavender shadows across the street and through the barred west windows of Cheyenne's Laramie County Jail. A year had passed since Charley Miller was sentenced. Deputy Harry W. Griffith went alone into the cell area and prepared for the nightly lockup by opening an aisle door to the lower tier of cells. His routine called for the removal of supper dishes at about five o'clock each afternoon. With no fellow deputy that day, Griffith called for prisoner William Parker's help. Parker, whose good conduct had earned him special privileges, immediately responded by retrieving cups, plates, and utensils from the adjoining cells. He then placed them in a tray near the main door. To let Parker exit with his load of dishes, Griffith removed the huge iron padlock and held it in his fist while swinging open the grated door with his other hand. As the trustee passed through, inmates William Kingen, Richard Johnson, and Charley Miller rushed in from around the corner. Kingen brushed Parker aside as he grabbed Griffith's arm. During their struggle, the nimble deputy broke loose and threw the heavy lock. It missed his assailant, but struck Parker a stunning blow that sent the metal tray and its contents crashing to the floor. With Kingen and Johnson at his heels, Griffith scrambled to the door into the courthouse hallway and, with his mouth glued to the peep-hole, yelled for help until Kingen's long fingers crushed those calls in the guard's throat. After dragging Griffith back to the middle of the aisle, Kingen pinned him to the floor. Using laces from an Indian prisoner's moccasins, Kingen tied a rag-wrapped broomstick into Griffith's mouth, gagging him. Kingen and Johnson next bound his hands and feet with a clothesline. After an unsuccessful search of the lawman's pockets, a disappointed Kingen exclaimed, "By god, boys! He has got no gun. That's too bad!"

Now Charley Miller came out of the cellblock carrying hats and coats as the other escapees relieved Griffith of his keys. "Don't harm the guard," warned Kingen. The three prisoners then returned to their cells and donned the extra clothing they had stashed for their well-planned flight. Beneath his jacket and greatcoat, Kingen wore "two heavy overshirts, good underclothes, two pairs of warm breeches beneath overalls and three pairs of socks." Anticipating the cruel wind's icy fingers, he also wrapped a black silk scarf about his neck and ears. He tied his firm-soled leather slippers to his feet with string. Like Kingen, the boy and the ex-soldier Johnson wore soft, low-cut, slip-on footwear over several layers of socks. Then they made for the exit. After struggling without success for about a minute with a stubborn lock in the jail door, they hurried to the front entry and went into the courthouse hall. At the outer door, Charley threw down the cumbersome bundles of blankets and extra clothes, but he kept their vital sack of food saved from past meals and grasped it tightly as they raced off into the darkness.

All through that New Year's night—January 1, 1892—the fugitives pressed on, but halted every few minutes for the exhausted, gasping Kingen.

Throughout their next day on the lam, the men struggled on. Charley lay down in the snow-covered grass beside Kingen each time the rancher took a break, but Johnson's constant nagging and their fear of the law's pursuit put them back on their feet. As light again

Deputy Harry Griffith was duped and pinned to the floor the night Charley Miller and his friends escaped from the Laramie County Jail. He had the last laugh, however: he served Miller his final meal, then escorted him to the gallows. (Wyoming State Archives)

turned to night, the disoriented trio looked back in confusion at the glow of Cheyenne's electric lights until Charley's instinct led them across some railroad tracks a few hundred yards below Archer Station. As they struggled down a glassy draw, Charley and his friends fought for footing in their smooth-soled jail shoes. Each awkward step on that frozen field, blotched with cattle dung, sapped their failing strength and left them gasping thin, frosted air until Kingen and Charley collapsed for the last time. Ice proved their undoing.

Only God knew that Charley lived; the cold had so chilled his blood that his pulse barely kept pace with his laboring lungs. In fact, a mirror near his mouth might not have found a breath. But the spark of life is so strong, and the spirit of survival so great, that even in his deep sleep he responded to the fear of death. CRACK!

Rancher R.S. Van Tassell's men found Charley Miller unconscious, freezing, and near death in a snowy field four days after he and two other prisoners escaped the Laramie County Jail on New Year's Eve, 1891. (Wyoming State Archives)

"For Christ's sake," Charley cried as he rolled up on his elbow; "Don't kill me!" The warning pistol shot from Al Lovell, a Hillsdale Land and Cattle Company wrangler, got the young killer's attention before "Captain" E.S. Smith, with two more of R.S. Van Tassell's hired hands, cautiously approached the boy and his dead companion. Helping Charley to his feet, Cuba Godfrey said, "You're pretty nearly a goner."

The boy replied, "I wish I was a goner." Godfrey and another cowboy walked him in a circle to stimulate his circulation, but Charley soon collapsed again.

Lovell had found the boy at about three-fifteen in the afternoon, January 2, while checking and oiling the windmills, but fearing for his safety, he raced back to the ranch for help. Captain Smith, searching that area for the outlaws, offered assistance.

Believing the boy might not survive the trip back to the ranch unless they hurried, Smith, Godfrey, and Frank Peterson loaded him into their cart before turning their attention to Kingen. After covering the dead man's head with a horse blanket, they tossed several spent cartridges near the corpse. This "wolf insurance," they believed, would repel predators with its gunpowder smell until they returned for the body.

Upon reaching Van Tassell's ranch, they carried limp Charley to the house and tucked him into a bunk. The ranch cook's tea, soup, and other liquid stimulants revived the boy's faint heartbeat while a fresh fire warmed his body. As they removed Charley's frozen clothes and made him relatively comfortable, they found in his belongings a harmonica and a small packet of songs, all neatly copied in his own hand on scraps of paper. "They were among his most valued possessions and consisted solely of metrical laudations of criminals, robbers, and thugs," claimed a reporter later. After lying unconscious for about two hours, the boy rallied and tried talking, but incoherently. Then his groans and gasps turned to silence until they revived him by bathing his head with water. "When will a doctor come?" he moaned, his mind wandering. He craved water, too, drinking incessantly when conscious.

Early the next morning, Sheriff A.D. Kelley and a small group arrived at the ranch and found Charley bundled in blankets and bison robes on a pallet by the roaring fire. Despite the comforts lavished on him, he continued vomiting "black, foul matter" and breathing with great difficulty. After breakfast Van Tassell's men hitched up a team and retrieved Kingen's body for a coroner's inquest at the rancher's home.

Following the proceedings the sheriff and his men hustled Charley—and Kingen's corpse—to Hillsdale, the nearest rail station, and through the crowd gathered there. After taking Kingen's body into the depot storeroom, they sewed it up in a tarpaulin for transit. Upon their arrival in Cheyenne that evening, they made their way through another even larger crowd and turned Kingen's body over to the undertaker. During his trip to the county hospital, Charley barely spoke above a whisper, but settled in upon arrival and slept most of that night.

Late the next morning, a reporter from Cheyenne's *Daily Leader* called on Charley and found him lying on a single bed. The boy's eyes, he said, "glared with a sort of vacant stare and he breathed apparently with great difficulty. His lips were blistered, his face and hands were chapped and tanned by the winds, and his feet were as black as a black cat in a dark alley on a foggy night."

Despite the boy's continued good care, the frostbite took its toll and the flesh died, so the following week Doctor Wyman amputated the toes of Charley's right foot.

At about the same time, the last jailbird in flight—Johnson—was caught on the open prairie three miles north of Pine Bluffs. Constable A.R. Robertson and his deputy, Harry Thomas, caught the black man as he rode toward town in a wagon with a Swedish farmer. Later Johnson said that after leaving Kingen and the boy in his wake, he walked the rest of that night. Finally, late the next afternoon, he stumbled into the cabin of a Swedish family some twenty-five miles north of Pine Bluffs. After they cared for him for several days, the old man offered to take him to the Pine Bluffs railway station. Authorities subsequently returned him to the Laramie County Jail to serve out his original sentence for "furnishing fire water to redskins."

A month later, Charley had recovered enough to appear before the Wyoming State Supreme Court. Standing with the aid of a chair, he listened stoically as Chief Justice Herman V.S. Groesbeck refused further delay of the boy's execution. Without showing emotion, Charley resumed his seat.

During his final month, the condemned youth wrote a bit about his misadventures and penned some bad, maudlin poetry, including an obscene rhyme on the flyleaf of his Bible. He also prepared special invitations to his execution for those he considered his friends. When *Daily Sun* reporter Ed Towse entered the county jail at lockup time on March 28, the boy handed him a note.

Laramie County Sheriff A.D. Kelley, who was out of town when Miller and his friends escaped, returned soon thereafter to orchestrate their capture and Miller's subsequent execution. (Wyoming State Archives)

> *As you have treated me fairly during my various troubles, I invite you to witness my execution April 22, 1892. It will be by hanging and at the court house in this city.*
> *Yours Truly,*
> *Chas. E. Miller.*

Towse quickly accepted the offer and thanked him for the acknowledgement.

Jail officials documented the crowds that would "flock to the jail nearly every hour in the day" for a glimpse at the prisoner, including "a great many women [who] persist in seeing Miller, much to that individual's discomfort." Despite the noise of some

The Union Pacific Depot in Cheyenne served as a makeshift mortuary upon the grim arrival of Miller's victims. (Wyoming State Archive)

150 curious visitors passing through the jail, Charley undoubtedly heard the carpenter's hammering as his scaffold rose inside the high stockade on the west side of the building. Although the public attention had invigorated him earlier, the boy failed physically and emotionally during the last week of his life as a haggard, haunted stare replaced his rare, forced smile.

During the final forty-eight hours of his life, Charley gave $2.50 to a fellow prisoner named Dwyer. The last of his money he shared with Johnson, his partner and survivor of that final and failed escape.

In the meantime, Sheriff Kelley tested an unusual self-hanging machine never before used in Wyoming. The water-powered, time-delayed mechanism beneath the scaffold would be visible to all. According to witnesses, "The automatic contrivance works well. Ed Lawler supplied the valves for the water weight adjunct. In trial the 100-pound block of wood used dropped in forty to sixty seconds after being placed on the trap...."

That afternoon, the sheriff's men lubricated the rope and fitted the restraining straps. And early that evening an amateur photographer stopped by the jail and took Charley's picture, promising him a copy.

The following day, Charley ate restaurant fare and that evening he played seven-up and chatted until midnight with his death watch, Deputy Sharpless. With less than twelve hours of life left, the boy went to bed and slept soundly until 6:20 A.M. on his final day—April 22, 1892.

About two hours later, Deputy Griffith brought a breakfast basket from the Capital Restaurant: eggs and coffee for the murderer. Father J.C. McCormack arrived at about 9:15 with news that the governor refused his clemency appeal for the second time. With all hope gone, the young man asked the priest for acceptance into the Catholic faith. The padre had refused his previous request for fear that, if the boy were reprieved later, he might change his mind and renounce his new creed. This time Father McCormack agreed and heard his confession before baptizing him. Suddenly courageous with his newfound faith, Charley repented for the first time since his capital crimes and caressed a crucifix as he prayed with the priest. In the meantime, Deputy Sharpless returned to the cell with a cutaway suit of fine black cloth, a pair of new shoes, a dark blue woolen shirt, and a black tie. The somber attire pleased Charley.

Attorney and Mrs. Taggart arrived at Charley's cell at 10:05. For the first time, the boy expressed gratitude for the lawyer's past aid. With tears in his eyes, he also thanked Mrs. Taggart for her efforts on his behalf. He told her, too, he "did not know there were such good women." In response, she offered to escort him to the scaffold, but Mr. Taggart dissuaded her.

As the countdown began, the halls of the jail filled. Outside, the police and guards controlled the growing crowd of fifteen hundred people, including some who assembled on the roof of the nearby Castle Dare mansion. Others climbed telegraph poles for peeks over the high fence as authorities concluded their tests of the mechanized death machine.

As the jailhouse clock chimed ten-thirty Charley seemed to panic again, but Mrs. Taggart and the priest calmed him by asking if

Herman V.S. Groesbeck, chief justice of the Wyoming Supreme Court, refused to delay Miller's execution. (Wyoming State Archives)

he wished to confess anything else. "No," he responded. Although he claimed remorse for his crimes against the St. Joe boys, he added nothing to his confession or courtroom testimony.

The tension mounted. At 10:55 the huge crowd in and about the courthouse became restless. His face flushed, Charley was visibly wilting under the mounting pressure so Mrs. Taggart and Father McCormack again tried to ease his agitation by having him repeat a litany of prayers. Ten minutes later Sheriff Kelley arrived and reminded everyone of their mission.

Finally, at 11:23, the small procession led the condemned boy into the sunshine at the foot of the stairs leading to the gallows some ten feet above. Sheriff Kelley led the way up the steps. Pale Charley clasped a large cross in both hands, but on his way to the noose, his face reddened and he clutched Father McCormack's arm for support. Deputies Wilkes and Griffith followed, with Attorney Taggart bringing up the rear as the group ascended the stairs. With all participants in place, the sheriff and Deputy Wilkes applied the straps as Charley again prayed in a clear, strong voice, "God have mercy on me. Jesus save me." Leather bracelets bound Charley's wrists. A thong went under his elbows. Still another firmly held his knees. The boy's eyes fixed upon the crucifix he carried and he moaned, "God have mercy on my soul." Repeating that prayer, he cocked his head slightly as if checking the braces of the wooden upright near his elbow. As his wandering gaze met the noose before his face, he implored God, "Please be quick." Observers who had closely followed the boy's trial and incarceration reported that even under the stress, his health seemed much improved. Even his complexion seemed clear and his eyes, glistening in the sun's light, turned from jailhouse grey to sky blue.

Upon command, the boy stepped toward the edge of the fatal trap. The sheriff caught the swinging noose, slipped it over Charley's head, and adjusted the knot at the base of his left ear. "Do you want me to stand right in the middle?" asked the boy.

"No," said the sheriff, "remain here for the present."

Moments later, at precisely 11:27, an official slipped a black cloth hood over Charley's head. The suspense now unbearable, the young man stepped forward onto a double-paneled trapdoor supported by a five-foot-long wooden two-by-four, hinged in the middle. That act, in turn triggered an inexorable chain of fatal mechanical movements. Under the scaffold, this action drew a cord over a pulley, plucking a plug from a water-filled gallon-sized tin can balanced from a fulcrum. A metal counterweight hung opposite it. Ironically, the mechanism resembled the scales of justice. Water spewed from the can. In a few moments, the now-heavier counterweight would drop and tug a cord, jerking away the hinged upright upon which Charley stood.

Sheriff Kelley, startled at finding his prisoner's feet unsecured, quickly tied a strap there. At that same time, beneath the hood, the boy cried in a muffled, high-pitched voice, "This rope is choking me!"

The mechanized trap of this execution device at the old Wyoming State Penitentiary is similar to that used to hang Charley Miller. It was patterned after one invented by a convict at the Colorado State Penitentiary. Because the condemned man's own weight set the machine in motion, an executioner was not needed. (Wyoming State Archives)

After the sheriff adjusted the knot and relieved the pressure, his prisoner sobbingly assured him it was "all right," and resumed his prayer: "God have mercy on me." Seconds passed while the trembling prisoner prayed and listened to the gurgling water as its flow shifted the balance between life and death. Thirty seconds … forty … fifty ….

Fifty-eight and three-quarters seconds. The upright support pole collapsed, the wooden panels swung open with a loud clatter, and the scaffold lurched as the weight of Charley's body snapped the lad's neck at the end of the rope some five feet below the platform. Then silence, broken only by the soft, creaking voice of the rope. No struggle ensued, although muscle contractions caused several slight tremors in Charley's legs.

During the next ten minutes, Doctor W.N. Hunt of the Laramie County Hospital and an assistant twice checked the boy's faint, still-beating pulse with a stethoscope. At 11:40, the doctor pronounced Charley dead—the first and youngest person ever legally executed in the state of Wyoming. The undertaker and his helpers placed the five-foot, four-inch corpse, its sinewy neck stretched slightly by the impact of its drop, into a plain black coffin lined with white cloth.

Poor Charley. His life lasted only seventeen years, nine months, and a fistful of days. A burial, hardly noticed, took place the next morning in an unmarked grave in Cheyenne's Lakeview Cemetery, the memory of Charley's crimes frozen in time.

❧ SOURCES CITED ❧ This telling of Charley Miller's story is based on documents from such primary sources as Laramie County Criminal Case File #3-827 *State of Wyoming v. Charles Miller* [District Court of the First Judicial District Court]; Wyoming Supreme Court Case File #2-96, *Charles Miller v. State of Wyoming*; the Laramie County Prison Calendar; and the correspondence files of Wyoming Acting Governor Amos W. Barber.

Secondary sources, particularly Cheyenne's *Daily Leader* and *Daily Sun*, were invaluable for they provided most of the dialogue and colorful narrative found here. U.S. state censuses for Kansas, New York, and Wyoming, and Phyllis Swanson's regional history titled *City of the Plains: A Story of Leonardville* (publisher not known, 1982) also were helpful in reconstructing some details.

All sources but the regional history can be found in the Wyoming State Archives in Cheyenne.

This chapter first appeared, in a slightly different form, in *True West* magazine, June 1997.

CHAPTER 24

WYOMING GIRL GUARD

THEY STEPPED IN TIME

TWENTY-FOUR PAIRS of sensible shoes marched as one across Keefe Hall's wood floor while spectators at the Merchants' Carnival in Cheyenne, Wyoming, watched admiringly. In the glow of Japanese lanterns, amidst banners and bunting, Wyoming State Guard Captain F.A. Stitzer led his "Maiden Guard" volunteers through their first public paces on October 22, 1889.

True to the mock-military spirit, the two dozen girls—collectively called "Company K"—were uniformed in light cream-colored dresses with black collars and sleeves. In their white-gloved hands they carried hand-carved wooden prop rifles. Formed just a month earlier by First Presbyterian Church ladies to entertain at their fall festival for local vendors, Stitzer's drill team dazzled the crowd with their civil (non-military) maneuvers, including the intricate formation of Latin and St. Andrew's crosses.

That show led to a repeat program on November 7 at the GAR (Grand Army of the Republic) Fair. Its proceeds helped Civil War Unionist veterans and their dependents survive that winter.

After a tune-up at Keefe Hall the following February 6, the girls went the next day to Greeley, Colorado, where they stepped smartly before an appreciative audience at the opera house. The receipts paid their travel expenses and benefitted the Greeley Presbyterian Church.

At the invitation of Wyoming State officials that spring, the group performed, too, for the GAR's national commander General Russell A. Alger and his party during their visit to Cheyenne. It would later serve as the guard of honor for the widow of General John A. Logan, a GAR founder, who accompanied the dignitaries.

Company H of the Wyoming Girl Guard stands in a brace in front of the State Capitol in Cheyenne. Perhaps the unit's greatest glory came on July 23, 1890, when it marched with its sister unit Company K to celebrate Wyoming's admission as the union's forty-fourth state. (Wyoming State Archives)

The repeated successes of Company K resulted in the formation of a second "Girl Guard" detachment—Company H—to participate in Wyoming's pending spring statehood festivities. Unlike its predecessor, Company H members drilled solely in military maneuvers according to the instructions of two Fort D.A. Russell Seventeenth Infantry officers: First Lieutenant George Ruhlen, post adjutant, and First Lieutenant Freeman V. Walker, assistant surgeon. Thanks to the unit's affiliation with the local Knights of Pythias, its captains carried swords on loan from that fraternal order.

To help raise funds for new uniforms—black broadcloth dresses faced with gold braid, white gloves, and regulation Army fatigue caps—the girls held a "dress drill and party" in mid-April featuring the Union Pacific Railroad's orchestra.

Perhaps the Girl Guard's greatest glory came July 23, 1890, in front of the State Capitol, where they joined a host of onlookers to officially celebrate the nation's acceptance of Wyoming as its forty-fourth state. Marching in the parade that followed, Captain Emma O'Brien's Company K guard of honor flanked a horse-drawn carriage bearing Wyoming's new state flag. At their heels, Captain Hattie Argesheimer and her Company H accompanied the "car of state." The ship-shaped float carried young girls costumed in red, white, and blue, each bearing a shield emblazoned with a star and the name of a previously admitted state. Next came two Shetland ponies pulling a buggy carrying the "Goddess of Liberty" and two lasses representing Idaho (the forty-third state) and Wyoming.

Despite rumors that officials had actually mustered Company H into military service for the statehood ceremony, no records substantiate that allegation and both Company K and H disbanded soon thereafter. However, nearly a century later, on October 25, 1989, women of Wyoming's Army and Air National Guard formed a contemporary "Wyoming Girl Guard" to honor their sisters and ensure that their spirits continue to march proudly through time.

❧ SOURCES CITED ❧ Although there are few readily available primary source materials, those interested in learning more about these exceptional women may at least view a Wyoming Girl Guard kepi (artifact #70.87.1) and wooden rifles (#70.87.2), and their accession records, at the Wyoming State Museum.

A wide variety of secondary source information, however, is available. Some of the best may be studied by contacting the staff historian of the Wyoming National Guard. T.A. Larson's article "Wyoming Statehood" in *Annals of Wyoming* (Vol. 37, No. 1), April 1965, also is an excellent primer on this subject.

This chapter first appeared, in a slightly different form, in the *Casper Star-Tribune*, May 18, 1997.

CHAPTER 25

GOVERNOR JOHN A. CAMPBELL

FRIEND OF FEMINISTS EVERYWHERE

CIVIL WAR HERO, United States assistant secretary of war, first governor of Wyoming Territory. Yes, John Allen Campbell achieved much in his relatively brief life of forty-five years. But many believe his most important achievement came on December 10, 1869, when he signed the legislative bill that granted women of Wyoming—and, ultimately, most of those throughout the free world—the right to vote and to hold public office.

Others suggest that his greatest show of courage came two years later when disgruntled majorities of the Territorial Senate and House of Representatives voted to repeal that law. It was saved only by Governor Campbell's veto. He reasoned:

It is simple justice to say that the women entering for the first time in the history of the country, upon these new and untried duties, have conducted themselves in every respect with as much tact, shrewd judgment, and good sense as men…and she has a right to claim that, so long as none but good results are made manifest, the law should remain unrepealed.

Further, he argued, suffrage in Wyoming would prevail because it "perfectly conformed to all of the other laws in relation to women in the Territory's statute books."

To override the governor's veto required a two-thirds vote of each house, but the legislators failed to marshal their forces, and the repeal bill succumbed. Historian Grace Raymond Hebard subsequently praised the bipartisan achievement, claiming "the Democrats [who controlled Wyoming's 1871 Legislature] gave the women their enfranchisement and the Republicans [specifically Governor Campbell] preserved that privilege" (see chapter 19: "A Source and Subject of Wyoming History").

Born in Salem, Columbiana County, Ohio, on October 8, 1835, Campbell attended public school before entering the newspaper business. With the outbreak of the War Between the States, he joined the Union Army on October 31, 1861, as a first lieutenant with the First Ohio Infantry, where he served as a "publicity writer." Thanks to his administrative talents, as well as his "gallant and meritorious service" in combat at Shiloh and Stone River in Tennessee, he reached the brevet rank of brigadier general in March 1865. Three years later, he became United States assistant secretary of war and, in April 1869, President Ulysses S. Grant made him governor of the new Wyoming Territory. While serving in that capacity, he married Isabella ("Belle") Crane Wunderly (anglicized from "Wunderlich") in Presbyterian services on February 1, 1872, in Washington, D.C. A baby daughter, named for Mrs. Campbell, blessed that union April 14, 1873.

Following two consecutive terms as Wyoming's governor (April 15, 1869 to March 1, 1875), he returned to the nation's capitol, where he served as an assistant secretary of state until, according to the *Cheyenne Daily Leader*, he became ill with an unnamed but "terrible disease...the origin of which he traced back to his army life." When "his mind became clouded and he was made unfit for mental work," friends gained for him a consulship at Basel, Switzerland, in hopes a change of scenery and climate might improve his health. Eventually, however, his condition further deteriorated, forcing his confinement in a Washington, D.C., asylum, where he died on July 15, 1880.

ᵇ SOURCES CITED ᵇ How better to get inside the mind of this exceptional leader than by reading "Governor Campbell's Diaries and Correspondence"? They can be found in files at the Wyoming State Archives (see MA 2411 – Box 2, Misc. Materials – Vault MSS #12). For a sense of the physical man, one should see his Civil War uniform (artifact #35.15.1), sash (#35.1.4),

John Allen Campbell, war hero and celebrated political figure, perhaps gained his most lasting fame when he signed into law a bill that gave Wyoming women—the first females anywhere—the right to vote and to hold public office. (Wyoming State Archives)

sword (#35.15.2a), and scabbard (#35.15.2b) maintained at the Wyoming State Museum.

Secondary source materials about his military career include the *Historical Register and Directory of the U.S. Army, 1789–1903* (Washington, D.C.: U.S. Government Printing Office, 1948). The *Wyoming State Blue Book*, Vol. 2 (Cheyenne: Wyoming State Government, 1974) and *History of Jury Service for Women* (Thermopolis, WY: Women's Business & Women's Professional Club, 1953) synthesize his public service in Wyoming, while "The Late J.A. Campbell," published in the *Cheyenne Daily Leader* on July 17, 1880, summarizes his life and death.

This chapter first appeared, in a slightly different form, in the *Casper Star-Tribune*, February 2, 1997.

CHAPTER 26

Alexander Hamilton Swan

KING OF THE CATTLE BARONS

And here let me draw a likeness… Cast your eyes upon a por-traiture of Uncle Sam and you have it. He was lank and gaunt and had a rather long face; was bearded like Uncle Sam; had gray hair and was knock-kneed. And those fine blue eyes! I can see them now.

THAT IS HOW Ferdinand W. LaFrentz, the first cashier of the Swan Land and Cattle Company, remembered his friend and boss, Alexander Hamilton Swan.

Regrettably, but for good reasons, others shared less charitable opinions of the cattle baron. John Clay, who succeeded him as head of the Swan Land and Cattle Company, called him a "reckless and slippery promoter." But love him or hate him, few can deny Swan's impact on ranching history.

Born November 24, 1831, in Green County, Pennsylvania, Alex grew up on the farm of his parents, Charles and Margaret (Barebry) Swan. At age twenty-two he moved west where he raised livestock for the next eighteen years in Iowa, Ohio, Kansas, and Colorado. Finally, in 1873, he landed in Wyoming where he bought a ranch at the head of Chugwater Creek in what is now Platte County. There with his brothers Thomas ("Black Tom") and Henry, and nephew Will F. Swan, he first established Swan Brothers. That fall he moved with his wife, Elizabeth, and their children William (born April 1862) and Louise (born September 1864) to Cheyenne where the Swans made their home for the next quarter century. (Alex had mar-ried "Lizzie" in 1858, but some believe he first married a woman named Anne McCullaugh.)

Alexander Hamilton Swan was often called "King of the Cattle Barons," but one detractor deemed him a "reckless and slippery promoter." In the end it mattered little because his empire crashed and he died of "softening of the brain." (Wyoming State Archives)

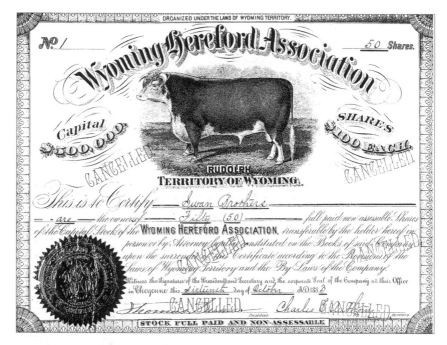

Wyoming Hereford Association officers issued this $5,000 Capital Stock Certificate No. 1 to the "Swan Brothers" on October 16, 1883. Alexander Hamilton Swan, who founded the Swan corporation, promoted the venture by adorning each such certificate with the profile of "Rudolph," his sixteen-hundred-pound, prize Hereford bull. The $3,500 that Swan paid to the critter's English owner that year topped any previous price paid for a Hereford in that country. (Wyoming State Archives)

During the next seven years, as the Swan Brothers livestock grew from 3,000 to more than 24,000 head, Swan became chairman of the Laramie County Commissioners, introduced purebred Hereford cattle to Wyoming's ranges, founded the Wyoming Hereford Association, and helped organize what became the Wyoming Stock Growers Association.

Then, in 1880, he pulled out of the Swan Brothers' business, formed a syndicate with Scottish capital, and started the $3.75 million Swan Land and Cattle Company, Ltd. Within five years, his holdings increased in value to $50 million as he ran cattle from Scottsbluff, Nebraska, to Fort Steele in Carbon County, Wyoming. In addition to owning a large Iowa farm and two cattle feedlots in

Nebraska, he founded what became South Omaha, Nebraska, and helped create Omaha's famed Union Stockyards.

Those good times ended, however, as Swan's finances foundered with the huge cattle losses during the blizzard of 1886. He "overexpanded his credit," claimed John Clay, "and pyramided his business to the point where bad weather, falling cattle prices, or any one of the problems common among cattlemen would bring him down." After his empire crashed the following May, he moved his family to Utah. There he engaged in mining until he died from "softening of the brain" on August 9, 1905, in a Provo asylum. His seventy-two-year-old wife, too ill to be at her husband's bedside, died only hours later. The following day, their children buried them side by side in an Ogden cemetery.

❧ SOURCES CITED ❧ One of Swan's legacies was the founding of the Wyoming Hereford Association. That organization's first stock certificate (MSS #537) is on file on shelf #1108 at the Wyoming State Archives' Collection Center South.

Enlightening information about Swan the man can be found in the "Recollections of Ferdinand W. LaFrentz" (MSS #579), which also may be reviewed at the Archives. There researchers may also read B.W. Allred's WHR [Wyoming Hereford Ranch]: *80 Years Young* (Kansas City, MO: American Hereford Journal, 1963); Chas. G. Coutant's "Mr. A.H. Swan, Cheyenne, Wyo," (vertical/subject files); "Alexander Hamilton Swan, Wyoming's Pioneer Cattle King" (MSS #582); "Hall of Fame Cites Fabulous Career of Alexander H. Swan," *Wyoming State Tribune*, March 9, 1960; and William H. Forbis's *The Old West: The Cowboys* (New York: Time-Life Books, 1973).

This chapter first appeared, in a slightly different form, in the *Casper Star-Tribune*, February 16, 1997.

CHAPTER 27

DR. LILLIAN HEATH

IN THE HANDS OF A HEALER

THE DESPONDENT sheepherder pressed the cold steel muzzle of his shotgun to the point of his chin. A split second later, a blast of buckshot tore away most of his jawbone as well as his upper lip, the tip of his tongue, and the end of his nose. Fortuitously, the burning gunpowder instantly cauterized the wound, thus preventing any major loss of blood. The bitter cold also averted potential deadly shock.

History does not record who found the fifty-three-year-old Englishman, nor how he came that November night in 1886 to Dr. Thomas G. Maghee in nearby Rawlins, Wyoming. We do know that after learning of the attempted suicide, the physician called for Lillian Evelyn Heath, his twenty-one-year-old nurse. As was their custom, she preceded the doctor to his office where she prepared the medical instruments. With everything in order, she retired to the drugstore across the street. In the meantime, Dr. Maghee arrived with his patient. After undressing the man and prepping him for surgery, the physician signaled with an oil lamp from the front office window for the nurse to return. Together they saved their patient's life and reconstructed his face so that he lived well into the next century.

His protégé's aptitude, intelligence, and skilled help during that and other procedures so impressed Dr. Maghee that he recommended her for formal medical training. Lillian Heath would soon become Wyoming's first woman physician and surgeon.

Lillian was one of two daughters of William A. and Calista Heath, born December 29, 1865, near Burnett Junction, Wisconsin, at her maternal grandfather Hunter's farm. Three years later the

Dr. Lillian Heath, Wyoming's first woman physician and surgeon, sometimes earned extra money as a fashion model in Denver. (Wyoming State Archives)

Heath family moved to Aplington, Iowa, where they remained until 1873 when they traveled by train into Wyoming Territory. Following brief stays at Cheyenne and Laramie, they moved four years later to Rawlins where they made their home temporarily at the Larry Hayes Union Pacific Hotel on the corner of Fifth and Front Streets. William Heath earned his family's keep by decorating passenger engines and their railcars. He painted "the bell, head lamps, and sand box gold with red and green stripes," said Lillian: "Parts of the locomotive were striped too! On the tender, he painted landscapes a foot and a half high by four feet long." Two years later he built his family a log cabin in Rawlins of salvaged telegraph poles. Finally, in 1881, he constructed a permanent two-story home for them at 111 West Cedar Street.

While Lillian and her sister Sylvia May—"Tib"—spent much of their teen years in that modest but comfortable abode, they also attended the local schools. Lillian so succeeded academically that at age sixteen, officials had her teach at New Carbon and later at Pass Creek. After receiving her high school diploma, she also taught grade school in Rawlins before enrolling in the University of Colorado at Boulder in 1890. The following year, based on his favorable experience with Lillian's nursing skills, Dr. Maghee endorsed her transfer to Keokuk, Iowa, where she began study at the College of Physicians and Surgeons. After earning her medical degree three years later, she specialized in obstetrics for three months at the college's local Mercy Hospital, a teaching center, before returning to Rawlins where she opened an office in the living room of her parents' home.

A sophisticated professional, Dr. Heath also knew when a down-to-earth touch was needed. An expectant mother's family called her the night of a masquerade ball to deliver a baby. The woman, Dr. Heath said,

> *... was a great, big, healthy girl and this was her first baby... [but she] wouldn't work on the delivery—just laid there hour after hour. Finally, I rolled her over and swatted her backside*

good three or four times. The delivery started soon after and she gave normal birth to a big, healthy boy without any trouble.

Dr. Heath also recounted her visit to another patient about fifty miles north of Rawlins:

The man had had kidney trouble but he was as bright and chipper as could be and not in bed at all when I arrived. I examined him and had him give me some specimens. It was too late and too far to return to Rawlins so I stayed the night. Later someone asked the old man how he felt and he replied: "Just fine; I just wanted to see what a lady doctor looked like!"

She also recalled the accident suffered by a former sweetheart, railroad engineer James Measures, and her treatment of him:

… the water glass in his engine cab broke. It was a gauge to tell how much water was in the oiler and it was under pressure. The cab immediately filled with live steam. James was burned on both arms from the shoulders down, his face, neck, and his back to the waistline. [The blisters on his arms were half an inch high.] The buckle on the back shoulder strap of his overalls was burned into his back. He was some time in finding his way out of the steam filled cab.

There was no hospital in Rawlins so he was bought to us. We put him on a bed here in the corner of the living room. Dr. Maghee prescribed mutton tallow, rendered out, strained, and whipped to a froth. Bandages were made from soft old sheeting, the whipped tallow was spread thin on the bandage out to the size of the area to be dressed. Every twenty minutes the bandages were wet with water. For weeks this procedure was kept up. He could do nothing for himself. He was hand fed and could have anything to eat. I stayed with him until midnight of each day and then railroad friends came and set up with him from midnight until six in the morning. Then I was back on duty. The only scar he had after this treatment was where the overall buckle burned his back.

Remarkably, she later claimed, "I never had a death during my medical practice!"

Respectable women of that time usually did not go out after dark without an escort, so to avoid gossip and potential trouble from drifters and drunks, Dr. Heath had a dress especially tailored to help disguise her decidedly feminine figure. She also concealed a brace of revolvers in two deep inner pockets, although she said she never fired them in anger.

To help maintain her skills, she regularly attended summer medical clinics in Denver, but during her free hours there she also modeled fashions at the Daniels and Fisher French Room. Store personnel, in fact, wanted her services full-time, "because she was a perfect '36' and wore a size 2-1/2 shoe and a size 6 glove. Therefore, dresses would not have needed altering."

At home in Rawlins, she also enjoyed hiking and joined the local bicycle club as its only woman member. Her other interests included service to the St. Thomas Episcopal Church. She also served as secretary to the Knights of Labor of the late 1880s and maintained active membership in the local Rebekah's Lodge as well as the Colorado Medical Society.

Her single years, although filled with personal and professional achievements, ended happily when she met handsome, mustachioed Louis J. Nelson, a young Norwegian-American painter and decorator. But when the Spanish-American War broke out during their courtship, Lou joined the military to serve his country. The couple finally reunited when Lou's unit discharged him, assigning him to the honor guard for President William McKinley attending the Trans-Mississippi Exposition in Omaha. They married there in the city overlooking the Missouri River on October 24, 1898, at the home of a mutual friend. Following the simple ceremony they returned to Rawlins, where they lived for all but three of their remaining years. (From 1909 to 1911 they owned and managed the Ben-Mar Hotel in Lamar, Colorado.)

During her later years, she and Lou became active in the United States War Veterans organization as well as the Wyoming

State Historical Society and its Carbon County chapter. And when Lou joined the B.P.O.E. (Benevolent Protective Order of Elks), Lillian became a Doe in the fraternal order's auxiliary.

Although she did not aggressively pursue her profession after 1909, her home office door stayed open to all who needed her healing hands—thanks in part to "Big Nose" George Parrott's skull, which she used as a doorstop and flowerpot. The outlaw's ivory-like cranium was a gift from fellow physician Dr. John E. Osborne, who later became governor of Wyoming (see chapter 37: "Four Times a Loser"). She also continued her medical studies and maintained her accreditation and license as a doctor until her death in the early morning hours of Sunday, August 5, 1962, at Rawlins Memorial Hospital. She had been hospitalized there since the previous February when she broke her hip for the second time.

And so, at nearly ninety-seven years of age, she joined her kin in their family cemetery plot to the sweet strains of her favorite musicians: coyotes and canaries.

❦ SOURCES CITED ❦ Neal Miller's undated and unpublished biographical sketch entitled "Lillian Heath, M.D.," as well as miscellaneous papers and materials from Lillian Heath's estate, are on microfilm (MA #1493) at the Wyoming State Archives. Those interested in this fascinating lady's life will also want to see her aluminum syringe kit (artifact #62.82.7) and leather surgical instrument kit (#62.32.8)—and their accession records—at the Wyoming State Museum. Her obituary, "Death Claims Dr. Lillian (Evelyn) Heath at Memorial Hospital Sunday," appeared in the *Daily Times*, Rawlins, Wyoming, August 7, 1962.

For more details on the first plastic surgery performed in Wyoming, readers should turn to David Cresson's "Plastic Surgery on the Wyoming Frontier," *Rocky Mountain Medical Journal*, Colorado Medical Society, Boulder, Colorado (Vol. 73, No. 4, 1976).

This chapter first appeared, in a slightly different form, in the *Casper Star-Tribune*, June 1, 1997.

CHAPTER 28

ROBERT D. MELDRUM

THE FINE ART OF MURDER

ONCE UPON A TIME, a mysterious marshal sketched life as he knew it in Old Wyoming, wove horsehair reins and rope, tooled fine leather, and, some speculate, murdered as many as fourteen men who stood in his way. Others give him credit for killing as few as seven.

What we do know is that Robert D. Meldrum drew a vicious gunfight scene as he cooled his heels in a Carbon County jail cell in Rawlins, Wyoming, awaiting trial. Which crime brought him down? Read on.

Meldrum said his life began 1861 in England; he soon emigrated to New York with his Scottish parents. He chose not to reveal details of his adolescence, but as a youth he surfaced in northern Colorado. He later bragged that, as a Pinkerton detective there, he and the infamous Tom Horn shot and killed two innocent men who they thought had hijacked horses from Rocky Mountain travelers.

Like a furtive flea, he popped up next in 1899 as a craftsman at a saddlery and harness repair shop in Dixon, Wyoming. Tough but slightly built at five feet, six-and-a-quarter, Meldrum returned to law enforcement there when Carbon County officials appointed him as deputy sheriff. In that position Meldrum caught Noah Wilkerson, an "accessory to murder," who had escaped from jail in Coleman, Texas. Their brief meeting ended when Meldrum's first pistol shot clipped the gunman's forehead and his second round ripped through the fleeing felon's back. The coroner claimed the outlaw never knew what hit him.

Robert D. Meldrum, a lawman who turned killer, may have left as many as fourteen dead men in his wake. His skill with leathercraft tools and an artist's pen, however, may even have exceeded his marksmanship. (Museum of Northwest Colorado)

Returning to Colorado, Meldrum was hired as a guard by owners of the Tom Boy Mine near Telluride, who later arranged his assignment as a deputy sheriff to break labor strikes. During the next five years, sandwiched between his killings of miners Olaf Thissel and David Lambert, Meldrum worked briefly in Boise, Idaho, where he wed a woman named Cora F., a reputed shrew with a son by a previous marriage. She later tired of his sodden lifestyle and left for parts unknown.

This untitled pen-and-ink sketch by Bob Meldrum illustrates a July 1898 gunfight between saloon proprietor James W. Davis and outlaw Jeff Dunbar that ended with Dunbar's death. Meldrum drew this picture in 1914 while imprisoned in the Carbon County Jail. (Wyoming State Archives)

By 1908, the man-killer Meldrum had returned to Wyoming, where the Snake River Stock Association hired him to patrol against rustlers. To assure his authority, county officials there, too, made him a deputy sheriff. (To supplement his income, he operated a ferry over the Little Snake River and managed the Finlayson Lumber Company in Baggs). Although increasing concern over Meldrum's rough-shod reputation spurred Carbon County executives to take back his badge, the people of Baggs seemed not to share that concern. They hired the hothead as their marshal, a position he held until January 16, 1912. That evening Meldrum arrested John "Chick" Bowen for disturbing the peace. When the rowdy drunk resisted, Meldrum shot and so wounded the cowboy that he died the next day.

A relatively swift trial for manslaughter ended with a guilty verdict, and Meldrum took up residence in the Carbon County Jail. (It was here that he drew the shootout scene shown here.) But legal maneuvers by the defense—and Meldrum's temporary flight

—delayed sentencing. Justice prevailed, however, on June 28, 1916, when the presiding judge sent the fifty-one-year-old defrocked peace officer to the Wyoming State Penitentiary in Rawlins, where he served time as inmate #2370. But thanks to influential friends and good behavior, Acting Governor Frank Houx restored Meldrum's freedom with a pardon on January 19, 1919.

Once out of prison, he moved to Wolcott where he opened a harness shop in which he also displayed his sketches and related fine art. He might have stayed there, too, had a fire not ravaged the establishment. With his last Wyoming roots destroyed, Meldrum again sailed free over the high plains like a tumbleweed torn by wind from the soil toward God knows where. Some suggest he joined a brother in Buffalo, New York. Others snort at that suggestion. Perhaps Meldrum had his reasons, as he did for his youthful years, to hide the truth.

❧ SOURCES CITED ❧ Several of Meldrum's fine ink sketches can be seen at the Wyoming State Museum. To view the one that depicts the shootout between James Davis and Jeff Dunbar, however, Meldrum's fans should inquire about artifact #A994.60 and its related accession records. Meldrum's criminal records (#2370) at the Wyoming State Archives also are "must-read" materials.

Many details on Meldrum's life in general were provided by Dan Davidson, curator of the Museum of Northwestern Colorado in Craig, Colorado. After his interview with me on March 11, 1997, he subsequently shared much information about and photos of Meldrum from his unpublished biography.

The following *Carbon County Journal* accounts tell of Meldrum's exploits: "Meldrum Sentenced" and "Bob Meldrum" (the latter an editorial, both August 29, 1913) and "Snake River Battles" (May 29, 1909). Additional related data may be found in John Rolfe Burrough's *Where the Old West Stayed Young* (New York: William Morrow & Co., 1962) and Harriet Fish Backus's *Tom Boy Bride* (Boulder, Colorado: Pruett Press, 1969).

This chapter first appeared, in a slightly different form, in the *Casper Star-Tribune*, March 30, 1997.

CHAPTER 29

WILLIAM F. "BUFFALO BILL" CODY

THE LEGENDS AND LIFE OF AN AMERICAN HERO

SOME CALL HIM "Colonel." His only true military officer ranks, however, were bestowed as militia commissions by the governors of Nebraska and Wyoming.

Others swear to his role as chief of scouts of the United States Army. Not so, but he served long and well with the Fifth Cavalry when appointed in that capacity by General Philip H. Sheridan.

And although he killed Cheyenne warrior Yellow Hair, historians claim their "hand-to-hand" duel actually took place with rifles from many yards apart. He scalped his fallen foe, too, but perhaps only after the other Indians had fled.

Still, even those skeptical of the mythic status of "Buffalo Bill" Cody do not hesitate to pay tribute to his *true* life and deeds.

Named William Frederick by his parents Isaac and Mary (Laycock) Cody at his birth on February 26, 1846, he was the fourth of eight children. Bill spent his first years on their farm near LeClaire, Iowa. Then at age seven he moved west with his family through Missouri to Kansas, where his father supplied hay and wood to Fort Leavenworth while trading with the Kickapoo Indians.

Following his father's death in 1857, the lad helped support his siblings and ailing mother by working as a herder and mounted messenger with the freight firm of Russell, Majors, and Waddell, organizers of the famed Pony Express (see chapter 38: Mare Mail"). Roughly four years later, he joined a wagon train bound for Fort Laramie, then spent several seasons trekking and trapping across the high plains and the Rocky Mountains.

In 1864 he enlisted in the Seventh Kansas Cavalry, a volunteer

William F. "Buffalo Bill" Cody, some say, made some dubious claims while others swear he surpassed even his greatest legends. (Wyoming State Archives)

Union regiment, and met Louisa Frederici in St. Louis, Missouri. The couple wed two years later and moved to Kansas where Louisa gave birth to Arta Lucille, Orra Maude, Irma Louise, and the Codys' only son, Kit Carson. After a stint as a stagecoach driver and a try at innkeeping in Leavenworth, he set out to make a living on the plains. He gained his "Buffalo Bill" soubriquet while supplying more than four thousand bison during eight months in 1867–68 to feed railroad construction workers. During the next eight years, mostly while serving as a Fifth Cavalry scout, he fought in nineteen

This "buffalo" coat, like so many legends of its wearer, is not what it seems. The garment, which sports a black-and-white striped, polished cotton lining and a leather tag stamped "Col. W.F. Cody," is simply sheepskin with its wool treated to resemble buffalo hair. (Wyoming State Museum)

conflicts and suffered one wound while earning America's highest award, the Medal of Honor.

In 1872, Cody guided Grand Duke Alexis of Russia on one of the century's most celebrated hunts on the plains of central Nebraska, with the ensuing publicity spurring the plainsman's acting career. Thanks in part to that newfound celebrity, he led a group of thirty-six Pawnee from Indian Territory and recruited some cowboys to form what later became his world-famous "Wild West Show." That first performance, however, took place as "The Wild West, Rocky Mountain, and Prairie Exhibition" on May 17, 1883, in Omaha. His partner that first season was Dr. W. F. Carver, a dentist and exhibition shooter, as their traveling road show crossed the country to acclaim. According to L.G. Moses, author of the section "Indians in Wild West Shows" for the *Encyclopedia of the American West*:

Cody's program for the first season of the show included a grand introductory march; a bareback pony race; recreation of a Pony Express ride and an Indian attack on a Deadwood Mail Coach; races by Indians on foot and on horseback; trick shooting by Cody and his partners; a horse race by cowboys; demonstrations of riding and roping, riding wild Texas steers, and roping and riding wild bison; and a "Grand Hunt" topped off by a "sham" battle with Indians.

Two years later, Annie Oakley became the first woman performer on his payroll when she and her husband-manager, expert marksman Frank Butler, joined the entourage. And still others found their way into Cody's show...and history: Bill Pickett, a black man who pioneered bulldogging as a rodeo event; Sitting Bull, the great Sioux chief; the "Congress of Rough Riders of the World"; and Buck Taylor, considered by many the first "King of the Cowboys."

The profits from that venture as it performed throughout Europe and the United States provided much of the capital for Cody's investments in ranching, mining, irrigation, publishing, and town building. His persona was also magnified by the many dime novels about his life and times. That image not only helped establish America's standards for manliness and morality thenceforth, it still feeds the public's imagination about the romantic West of yesteryear.

Cody's show lasted some thirty years, but eventually its profits dwindled. Despite poor health, debt forced Cody to continue performing through 1916 with other entertainment groups. On January 10, 1917, he died in Denver. Despite competing claims for his body from Wyoming and Nebraska, the state of Colorado won out, and its people buried the "Scout of the Plains" beneath two tons of concrete and a half-ton of steel rail on Lookout Mountain.

❧ SOURCES CITED ❧ Among all the Wyoming State Museum artifacts that once belonged to Buffalo Bill, perhaps one of the most interesting is the faux bison hide overcoat made of wool (#81.44.1). Its accession records explain how it came into his possession.

Much material was provided in a March 17, 1997, interview with Paul Fees, who is not only one of the most knowledgeable experts on Cody, but who served at that time as curator of the famed Buffalo Bill Historical Center in Cody, Wyoming.

To learn about the highlights of Cody's life, readers can turn to his biography, by Paul Fees and G. Moses, in the *New Encyclopedia of the American West* (Charles Phillips and Al Axehod, eds., New Haven, CT: Yale University Press, 1998) as well as Don Russell's *The Lives and Legends of Buffalo Bill* (Norman, OK: University of Oklahoma Press, 1960) and Paul Hedren's *First Scalp for Custer* (Glendale, CA: Arthur H. Clark Co., 1980).

This chapter first appeared, in a slightly different form, in the *Casper Star-Tribune*, April 27, 1997.

CHAPTER 30

LUKE VOORHEES

A GRAND, GILT LIFE

Having chased the sun along the Cheyenne–Black Hills Stage Line's route, the ironclad Concord coach with its load of Deadwood gold swayed to a dusty stop at Canyon Springs Station.

When the stock tender who usually helped with the seven-minute change of horses failed to show, one of the guards jumped down from his high perch to chock the wheels. Suddenly a hail of lead from ambush ripped his left arm and tore through his chest. Another guard and a passenger fell dead from bullet wounds while a third defender, stunned by a glancing shot, slumped in his seat. By using the wounded stock tender as a shield, the outlaws held at bay a fourth guard and the driver. They escaped with loot worth more than $27,000 in a strongbox. That September 26, 1878, crime near what today is known as Four Corners in Wyoming's Weston County proved to be the worst loss suffered by Luke Voorhees's fledgling business. But it did not hold him back; in fact he would later be entrusted with the Territory's entire treasury.

Born near Belvidere, New Jersey, on November 28, 1834, Voorhees moved to Michigan two years later with his parents. At age twenty-two he left home and worked his way west across Kansas to Colorado where, beginning in June 1859, he prospected in the Clear Creek area. His mining interests took him on to Alder Gulch in Montana in 1863. The next year he made his way into Canada where he found gold on the Kootenai River of northwest British Columbia.

Returning to the United States, he saw the last spike driven on May 10, 1869, uniting the Union Pacific Railroad and the Central

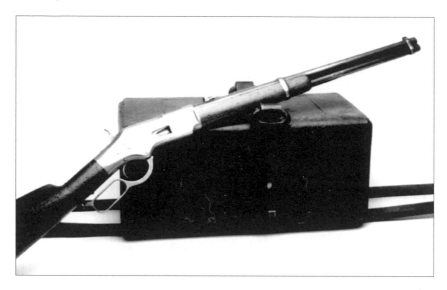

Cheyenne–Black Hills Stage Line guards, armed with weapons like this 1866 Winchester/Henry repeating rifle, protected gold and other valuables shipped in this strongbox. Bolts through the metal bands at the base of the hand-wrought, cast-iron or steel box secured the double-locked container to the stagecoach. Some believe the seven notches carved into the butt of this .44-caliber gun count the many Indians and/or outlaws who were its victims. (Wyoming State Museum)

Pacific Railroad tracks at Promontory, Utah. Five years later at Salt Lake City after investing heavily in the cattle industry, he married Florence Celia Jenks, with whom he had a son, George.

In March 1876 the Voorhees family moved to Cheyenne where he organized and managed the famed Cheyenne–Black Hills Stage Line on behalf of the Gilmer, Salisbury and Patrick firm. Through the heart of Indian country, Voorhees built change stations about fifteen miles apart and equipped the line with four- and six-horse Concord coaches. The line required three hundred custom-harnessed horses and string teams to freight forage and supplies. The 300-mile route extended from Cheyenne to Chugwater, Fort Laramie, and Rawhide Buttes, crossing the Running Water (Niobrara River) about a mile and a half west of Lusk. From there it continued to Hat Creek Station, a former frontier military post, then on to the Cheyenne River and finally to Custer City and Deadwood

Luke Voorhees, who organized the famed Cheyenne–Black Hills Stage Line in 1876 and managed it on behalf of the firm Gilmer, Salisbury and Patrick, was the oldest Wyoming pioneer at the time of his death in 1925. (Wyoming State Archives)

in Dakota Territory. Continuing day and night, with stops only for meals and changes of horses, the journey took slightly more than three days.

Stages left both Cheyenne and Deadwood daily, carrying mail, small parcels, and passengers. Voorhees usually shipped gold by armored six-horse coaches, under guard of four to six heavily armed shotgun messengers.

On February 19, 1887, eleven years after the first coach left the Inter-Ocean Hotel in Cheyenne, the last one departed that location for its final trip into the Black Hills.

Then Voorhees's cattle investments failed, but he went on to start the company that built the first gas works in Cheyenne, as well as the community's first streetcar service. With his appointment a decade later as the first Wyoming territorial treasurer, Voorhees became the first official to work in the then-new Capitol building. His bright career gained still more luster in May 1913 when President Woodrow Wilson appointed him as receiver of public monies and disbursing agent of the United States Land Office in Cheyenne.

Luke Voorhees was Wyoming's oldest pioneer at the time of his death, his obituary read. On January 16, 1925, he succumbed to pneumonia at home in Cheyenne, aged ninety-three. Following Episcopal church services the following day, his family buried him at the local Lakeview Cemetery.

❧ SOURCES CITED ❧ Those who know this story of the Cheyenne–Black Hills Stage Line robbery may shiver at the sight of one if its original strongboxes (artifact #73.44.22) at the Wyoming State Museum. Curious viewers will also want to study the related accession papers on file there.

As for the robbery itself, details can be found in Agnes Wright Springs's "The Canyon Springs Robbery" as published in the *Frontier Times*, December 1957-January 1958, and in "Details of Cold Springs Stage Robbery Are Told by Scott Davis," *Lusk Herald*, February 25, 1932.

To gain some understanding of the life and times of Luke Voorhees, readers may turn to the following: "Stage Ride Filled with Thrills in Early Days," *Wyoming Eagle*, July 28, 1939; "Pioneer Stage Driver to Be Buried Sunday," *Casper Daily Tribune*, January 17, 1925; and "Luke Voorhees, Widely Known Wyoming Pioneer Dies Friday," *Wyoming State Tribune*, January 17, 1925.

This chapter first appeared, in a slightly different form, in the *Casper Star-Tribune*, April 13, 1997.

CHAPTER 31

VERNA KEYES

A BISON ON HER BANNER

NEARLY A HALF CENTURY after the dream, Verna Keyes claimed she still clearly recalled her vision that summer night as well as what she did the next morning. With the sun's first light, she rolled from bed, put pen to pad, and drew the silhouette of a bison encompassing the dark blue circle of Wyoming's State Seal. That design won first place in the Daughters of the American Revolution's (DAR) 1916 state flag contest. Verna was just out of college at the time.

The following January 31—despite lobbying for the Democrats' donkey, the Republicans' elephant, and the Bull Moose party's namesake—the fourteenth State Legislature adopted her twenty-dollar-prize-winning entry as the basis for Wyoming's banner. Before that ensign flew over the statehouse, however, one of Verna's competitors forced a key change in its design.

Because the bison once roamed freely over the plains, Verna believed he "should so fly on the flag" and she pointed him to the right; that is, downwind—away from the flagpole. DAR State Regent Dr. Grace Raymond Hebard, who had originated the idea of the competition and entered a sketch of her own, strongly disagreed. The scholar and historian insisted that, since the bison keeps his nose to the wind, his image must face in that direction; that is, to the left. When the first official Wyoming state flag was made, Hebard's will prevailed, because "few questioned or crossed her," said Verna (see chapter 19: "A Source and Subject of Wyoming History").

Verna was born, appropriately enough, in Buffalo, Wyoming, on August 16, 1893. She and her younger brother Parke attended

Verna Keyes displays the flag based on her prize-winning design in the Daughters of the American Revolution's 1916 contest. (Wyoming State Archives)

public school near where their parents, Wilbur Parke and Estella (Ferguson) Keays, had settled some years earlier. Verna later accompanied a girlfriend to Cleveland, Ohio, where she attended high school while living with the chum and her parents. After earning her diploma, she moved to Illinois where, at age twenty-two, she graduated with honors in design and decorating from the Art Institute of Chicago.

Returning to Wyoming, she married Arthur Charles Keyes —whose surname almost matched her own—on June 1, 1921, and settled in Casper. Daughters Elizabeth and "Polly" (Priscilla) were born, respectively, in 1922 and 1925. Following Arthur's death twenty-six years later, Verna remained in the Casper home that she designed. On October 31, 1982, she died at age eighty-nine in the

Natrona County Memorial Hospital. But in the form of a bison on a banner, her spirit still flies over Wyoming.

❧ SOURCES CITED ❧ I thank Verna Keyes's only surviving daughter, Polly Newell of Bristol, Tennessee, for sharing with me, via phone on May 12, 1997, many memories of her mother's life. I have also had the pleasure of viewing Verna's prize-winning watercolor, ink, and gouache drawing at the Wyoming State Museum (artifact #A19.45.01) entered in the 1916 Daughters of the American Revolution flag contest.

Perhaps the most authoritative source about the Cowboy State's pennant is Verna's own article on that subject: "The Origin of the Wyoming State Flag," as published in the *Casper Chronicles* (Casper, WY: Casper Zonta Club, 1964). Additional data can be gained from Carol Crump's "Wyoming's Betsy Ross," *Casper Star-Tribune*, April 24, 1994; Linda Dougherty's "Earliest of State's Flags Recovered," *Casper Journal*, November 2, 1982, and Sandra Booth's "Designer of State's Flag Dies," *Casper Star-Tribune*, November 1, 1982.

This chapter first appeared, in a slightly different form, in the *Casper Star-Tribune*, June 10, 1997.

CHAPTER 32

Wyoming's Paleo-Indians

"SPANISH DIGGINGS"

A DREAMER THINKS HE hears sharp raps, taps, and muffled voices float from the sage-covered hills. In search of those sounds, his mind's eye seeks and imagines brown-skinned men with straight dark hair and raven eyes. Hunched in the parched grass, they chip chunks of lavender and gold-hued stone into crude tools, spear points and knife blades with which to hunt and make war.

And there is more easily imagined by the dreamer. But for the realist to see this scene at the "Spanish Diggings"—the primitive quarries in a 400-square-mile tract on the North Platte River—he must let his mind run wild. Race back, in fact, to the Ice Age when aborigines crossed the Bering land bridge to this continent.

Around 12,000 B.C., their ancestors followed herds of bison, mammoth, and other game to this land we call Wyoming. Although they faced a colder clime, the land they saw looked much as does today. And in what became Wyoming's eastern counties of Niobrara, Goshen, and Platte—especially near present-day Hartville—they found quartzite from which they made hide scrapers and heads for hoes and hammers. The edged implements they made from the crystalline substance stayed keen far longer than those fashioned from many other materials.

To reach that treasured stone, they used bones, antlers, and sharp sticks to scratch holes, averaging twenty-eight feet in diameter, as deep as thirty feet. After mining out each site, it seems they filled it with what they dug from the new hole they began next to it. Collecting the stone, they hauled it in baskets to their homes of hide.

Crude stone tools found at the "Spanish Diggings" include scrapers, points, blades, drills, and mauls. Hans Gautschi of Lusk, a Standard Oil dealer, acted as guide for several early archaeological expeditions into the area. He later cemented some collected artifacts into the low rock wall at the base of a small log cabin behind his filling station. (Wyoming State Archive)

There they struck off shards from which they formed into the tools and weapons they needed to survive in those ancient times.

Given the numerous excavations throughout the ten- by forty-mile area, experts reason such progress would not have been possible if the miners had also had to hunt for themselves. Therefore, they believe others took on that task. Such evidence suggests, too, that by cooperating, specializing, and dividing their labors, those same aborigines not only improved on the tools of their forebears, but they also pioneered the first organized technological enterprise in Wyoming.

Addison "Ad" A. Spaugh, an early rancher of Manville, Wyoming, is credited with discovering this archeological wonder in 1879 on his own property. The following summer when cowboys J.L. Stein and William Lauk viewed the open pits, they believed them to be the work of Spanish conquistadors prospecting for gold. Although they called the area "Mexican Mines" or the more familiar "Spanish Diggings," there is no proof that early explorers from those lands ever ventured this far north. Today the area is still bounded on the south and west by the North Platte River while state highways 20 and 85 skirt it to the north and east.

According to scientists, the type of artifact found in the Hartville area and the presence of piles of this type of stone suggest quarrying activities took place as early as the paleo-Indian period at the end of the last Ice Age.

❧ SOURCES CITED ❧ After viewing at the Wyoming State Museum some of the many points, scrapers, and blades (artifacts #23.3.1–69) that have been found at the Spanish Diggings, I interviewed Wyoming's State Archaeologist Mark Miller in Laramie about the significance of such items and the site itself. Our conversation took place on May 19, 1997.

For a quick read on those subjects, I recommend Mae Urbanek's "Stone Age Industry in Wyoming," as published in the *Annals of Wyoming* (Vol. 28, No. 2), October 1956, as well as *Wyoming: A Guide to Historic Sites* (Cheyenne: Wyoming Recreation Commission, 1988).

This chapter first appeared, in a slightly different form, in the *Casper Star-Tribune*, June 29, 1997.

CHAPTER 33

JAMES WILLIAMS

ESCAPE FROM THE GREYBAR HOTEL

JAMES WILLIAMS, Convict #426, Wyoming State Penitentiary, Rawlins, Wyo.—Date Received: April 24, 1899. From: Uinta County. Date of Sentence: April 21, 1899. Term: 5 years. Crime: Grand Larceny. Age: 23. Nativity: Ireland. Occupation: Barber and stone cutter. Height: 5' 6". Weight: 134 pounds. Complexion: Medium. Hair: Dark brown. Eyes: Hazel. Religion: Protestant. Education: Common. Habits of Life: Moderate. Marks, Scars & General Remarks: Spot scar, left side neck. Cut scar, back of head. Tattoo left arm. Naked woman, just opposite head of woman, vax [vaccination] scar. Tattoo, right arm, woman's head. Over it, flags and eagle, red and blue ink. Cut scar palm of right hand. Light brown birth mark, right buttock.

⁓

For several months, Williams's behavior seemed unusually odd, if not downright crazy. Apparently concerned for the health of his charge, prison physician Harry S. Finney convinced warden J.P. Hohn to move him to the vacant but secured third floor of the Wyoming State Penitentiary administration building. There, during the day, Williams roamed the empty Women's Ward at will; at night a guard locked him into a steel cage.

But at 11:35 P.M. on Friday, June 5, 1903, James Williams slipped his cell and the room with the aid of a key he had apparently whittled from a piece of wood. Entering the adjacent prison chapel, he made his way through an opening over the gallery and onto the roof. With the aid of a rope made from blankets, he lowered himself to the ground, thus claiming the distinction of

James Williams, convict #426, became the first criminal to escape Wyoming's state penitentiary in Rawlins. On June 5, 1903, having whittled a key from a piece of wood, he slipped from his cell into the prison chapel, made his way through an opening in the roof, and lowered himself to the ground with a rope made of blankets. (Wyoming State Archives)

This cellblock of the Wyoming State Penitentiary was home to some of America's most feared criminals for nearly eighty years. On December 17, 1901, when warden J.P. Hehn and his guards moved the first group of forty prisoners into this facility, it was designed to hold a maximum of 198. (Wyoming State Archives)

being the first person—but alas, not the last—to escape from that prison.

His freedom ended, however, the following Wednesday night when Carbon County Deputy Sheriff C.E. Dodge caught him on W.A. Clark's ranch near Dixon.

Had he not flown the coop, Williams could have left the pen a free man only sixty-five days later, having earned "good time" at a rate of two and a half days per month. Regrettably, what he lacked in patience he had already made up for in greed. His crime? Four and a half years earlier, he and two cronies—John Holloway and W.H. Montaziahlo—robbed Isadore Kastor's men's store in Evanston of more than four hundred dollars' worth of clothing, accessories, and watches. That felony gained Williams and his cohorts five-year reservations in Rawlins's infamous "Greybar Hotel."

Following the failed "French leave," authorities returned their prisoner to the solitary cell on the third floor to finish his original sentence. About two months later, Williams found liberation—but not the kind he so desperately sought. On August 17, as the hour approached midnight, his odd behavior lured E.B. Goodson to the door of his cell where the prisoner grabbed his waistband. During the ensuing struggle for the guard's gun, a fired bullet struck Williams square in his forehead, knocking him back and onto his bunk. Despite a doctor's care, he died where he fell three and a half hours later.

When his family in New York failed to respond to Warden Hehn's notification of death, authorities buried Williams on the following Thursday, August 20, in the prison's peaceful cemetery.

❧ SOURCES CITED ❧ The prison records of convict #426, James Williams, are maintained in the Wyoming State Archives. For more about Williams's attempted escape there is no better source than the *Rawlins Republican* newspaper accounts: "Convict Escapes," June 6, 1903; "Convict Caught," June 13, 1903; and "Killed in Cell," August 19, 1903.

Two publications with more information are Robert A. Murray's "History of the Wyoming State Penitentiary in Rawlins," as published in *Best Scene*, Wyoming State Penitentiary, Rawlins, Wyoming, (Vol. 27, No. 2), Winter 1981; and a pamphlet entitled "Friends of the Old Pen" (Vol. V, No. 3), July-September 1996.

Although they are unrelated to the Williams case, several items at the Wyoming State Museum—contraband knives and a con's "escape sandals"—make it easy to imagine a guard's concern upon finding weapons hidden in a prison cell.

This chapter first appeared, in a slightly different form, in the *Casper Star-Tribune*, July 20, 1997.

CHAPTER 34

Fred Ells

SUNRISE ON THE GLORY HOLE

F ATE CAN BE AS STRANGE as it is unpredictable. Take Fred Ells, for example. He planned to be a mechanical engineer and studied for years to do that job. But such was not his lot. Instead, he today owns a ghost town—but one whose future may yet affect the lives of many, as Ells sees it.

Although he might have learned of his inheritance in the papers of his late father, a Greeley-based entrepreneur, Fred was surprised when a stranger called him many months after the elder Ells's death in the early 1990s. Interest-bearing notes, secured by tax payments on the real estate, made Fred the unlikely heir to Eureka Canyon and Sunrise, a once boom, now bust burg in east-central Wyoming.

Although stunned by the caller's tempting offer to buy that property, Fred deferred. Instead, he visited the 1900-acre site in Platte County, some six miles north of Guernsey. There, upon entering the idyllic gulch, he found an Eden of wild flora and fauna that touched his heart and stirred his imagination. He also found a fierce, raw 44-acre wound—averaging 650 feet across—in the floor of his valley. Perplexed by what he saw, his mind played with that puzzle as he studied the site's history. What he learned put an end to his peripatetic past and gave his life a mission.

Sunrise's story began, it is believed, in ancient times when indigenous peoples collected from that place the greasy, bright-red hematite (Latin for "rock that bleeds") that they used for decorative body paint. Not until about 1880, when local rancher Henry T. Miller learned of the presence of copper in the soil, did the general public pay much attention to the place. When the mineral's vein

Sunrise, Wyoming, a Colorado Fuel and Iron Corporation company town, buzzed in its prime years (1900–35) like a veritable beehive as its workers and boxcars extracted ore there from the "Glory Hole," the largest open-pit ore mine west of the Mississippi. (Wyoming State Archives)

petered out, however, Miller moved deeper into the canyon and hired a crew to open the "Glory Hole."

Toward the end of that decade, the Colorado Fuel and Iron Corporation (CF&I) moved in and not only bought Miller's land, but also acquired mining claims from others in the region. The following year, the firm built a company town there called Sunrise—so named, it is said, because its residents could stand on the rim of its canyon for a fine view of each day's first light. And CF&I attacked the site with a vengeance that turned the Glory Hole into what became the world's largest open-pit iron mine west of the Mississippi.

During the first four years, the miners tore the rich ore from the soil with steam shovels, then moved it by rail up the wall of the crater. In 1904 they dug an L-shaped shaft next to the pit so that ore could be moved horizontally before being lifted vertically in buckets to the surface. Both the train and lift remained in use until 1921 when the small locomotive could no longer pull its load from the ever-deeper crater.

Surface mining ceased there twenty years later as CF&I's engineers introduced the more sophisticated "slusher level block caving" technique to extract the ore. With this method, they undercut large blocks of ore, causing the materials to cave. The fall and impact at the bottom of the pit broke the mass into bits small enough to be scraped into rail cars, then moved to the shaft for hoisting to the surface.

But rising labor costs in the Unites States, as well as the availability of cheaper, rich-and-ready iron ore from other countries, took its toll. In 1980 CF&I stopped its mining operations at Sunrise. Nine years later, the firm sought federal bankruptcy protection and tried to transfer the Sunrise acreage to the State of Wyoming, but state officials filed a disclaimer of interest on the property. In the meantime, Fred Ells continued to pay its property taxes and eventually acquired clear title to the land.

But what about the future of this now-deserted town? If Fred Ells has his way, the sun may never set on Sunrise. While encouraging public support to heal his land, he works to establish a museum that preserves the heritage of those who mined its wealth. He also hopes to open an "Environmental Center for Cultural Change" there so that, in Fred's words,

> ... the descendants of those who made Sunrise's history, as well as those who soiled their nests elsewhere, may come to the valley. There, perhaps, they will reflect, study their mistakes as well as learn how to develop and preserve America's natural resources in a more sensible way.

❧ SOURCES CITED ❧ Interviews with two experts on the Sunrise Mine provided my primary information about this subject. On May 27, 1997, I met with Fred Ells, who owns and lives on the property, while my second meeting took place soon thereafter with Ed Francis of the State of Wyoming's Abandoned Mine Land Office in Cheyenne.

Several excellent secondary sources include an undated pamphlet published by the CF&I Steel Corporation that offers *Facts About the Sunrise Mine* and Phillip J. Mellinger's "Frontier Camp to Small Town," *Annals of Wyoming* (Vol. 43, No. 2, Fall 1971). Additional facts and colorful details about the mine may be found in the following newspaper stories: "Sunrise Mine, 86 Years Old, Rich in Iron," *Casper Star-Tribune*, March 26, 1967; "Sunrise Only Town Built on Hematite," *Cheyenne Daily Leader*, June 19, 1908, and "Mine Dumped on Wyoming," *Wyoming Tribune-Eagle*, September 12, 1993.

This chapter first appeared, in a slightly different form, in the *Casper Star-Tribune*, August 3, 1997.

CHAPTER 35

Francis S. Brammar

"ONE-SHOT" BRAMMAR

Like "Chicken Man," a radio hero of yesteryear, he was "Everywhere! Everywhere!"

Just about anyone living in Cheyenne in the late 1970s remembers the gaunt, gangling "Bram," wild white hair weathervaning in the wind, lugging his camera down the street on his way to a photo shoot. Others recall his daily treks, sans coat and hat, to the Mayflower Café where, like a winter-worn corn stalk, he slouched over tea and toast. Despite his celebrity, however, even those who claimed his friendship acknowledge that they never really knew him.

What they do know is that for nearly a half-century photographer Francis S. Brammar, like the legendary Tom Swift and his wizard camera, trapped images of his times within his magic box. Presidents and generals, pinup beauties and cowpokes, socialites and clerks, kids with their pets. Their smiles and warts were frozen by his lens. His finest work also caught their spirit, their compassion, their *joie de vivre*. The sheer scope of his vast visual history of his community—44,000 negatives—astonishes even his staunchest admirers. But much of Bram's life was neither so memorable nor so successful.

The bushy-browed Bram was a very private person despite his high visibility. Some claim, unkindly, that he had no choice; he usually reeked of the acrid photo-processing chemicals in which he worked. Even most of his intimates did not know the basic details of his life.

Francis was born on April 23, 1900, in Wadsworth, Nevada, to Archibald and Sydia Steel. His parents separated, however, and years later Sydia married Ritner G. Brammar, a traveling salesman. The family moved to Denver where Francis attended elementary school and South Denver High School. In 1916 the family moved to Cheyenne where the boy's stepfather managed the Jewel Tea Company from his home.

After graduation from Cheyenne High School in 1919, Bram apparently clerked in a local paint store where he earned enough to buy a camera, a 4x5 Graflex, and began taking pictures as a hobby. That fall he enrolled at the University of Wyoming in Laramie, but the puckish prankster quit after one year.

Bram spent at least part of the next three years working for the Union Pacific Railroad, but in 1924 he enrolled at the Chicago branch of the New York Institute of Photography. There he found his niche. So quickly did he learn what he had not already taught himself that the faculty asked him to join the staff. His responsibilities included teaching still and motion-picture photography.

In 1926 while Bram was covering a Eucharistic convention in the Windy City, he was offered a job with the famed Hearst-Pathe Company of Hollywood. Accepting the offer, Bram packed his bags and returned to Cheyenne to visit his family before moving to the movie mecca in California. Once back on the high plains, however, his love of the great open spaces was revived. Then a fateful turn in his feuding parents' relationship dramatically changed his life: his stepfather deserted his mother in July 1926. Bram cancelled his California plans.

Faced with supporting himself and his mother, Bram struggled as a clerk until 1928 when he landed a proofreading job with the Tribune Publishing Company. About a year later he joined the *Wyoming Tribune* newspaper's reportorial ranks and married a gorgeous redhead named Dolores. Although nothing is known of her background or how they met, given Bram's unabashed passion for posing beautiful women, she may have been one of his many cheesecake models.

His next job was with a local etching and engraving company, which was taken over in 1932 by publisher Tracy McCraken to support his fledgling *Wyoming Eagle*. In return for his work as a photographer and technician, Bram received a small weekly stipend plus lab space and supplies.

Francis S. Brammar, the photographer who earned the soubriquet "One-Shot" for his "point and snap" technique, chronicled Cheyenne's history with his ever-present 35 mm Leica camera. (Wyoming State Archives,)

The lack of information about Bram's life during the next six or seven years suggests it was relatively uneventful. Recollections from business associates such as Bernard Horton, however, share insight into Bram's character and work ethic. The *Wyoming Eagle* editor recalled: "We never quite figured out Bram's working hours. Once when we asked him about them, he replied, 'I do not believe in working hours for newspaper men. I don't believe any newspaper man who is worth a damn should be confined by set working hours.'"

Nor is much known about the personal life of the enigmatic Bram during that period except that Dolores left him in 1940 because of his roving eye and suspected philandering. He apparently

Children at play must have brought much joy to Francis Brammar's life because he took so many fine photos of them. In fact, Brammar's lens had few peers when it came to capturing the cheerful and seemingly spontaneous play of such unidentified youngsters. (Wyoming State Archives)

found solace, however, in his own Walden: a Spartan apartment on Carey Avenue. With the stoic yet observant nature of a Henry David Thoreau, his philosophical mentor and muse, Bram witnessed the next twenty years of Cheyenne news through the viewfinder of his camera.

By 1960 Bram had become a devotee of the miniature camera and he began shooting almost exclusively with a Leica. It seems clear to students of his work that he emulated such pioneer photojournalists as Alfred Eisenstadt and Henri Cartier-Bresson in honing his "spot news" skills. His friend and associate Red Kelso said Brammar was one of the first press photographers to switch to 35mm film at a time "when even the slickers in the big cities were still using Speed Graflexes." The small-format camera was not only more convenient, it increased his working speed. Dubbed "One-Shot Bram," a nickname from which he seemed to derive satisfaction, he boasted, "I never had to take it but once." His unorthodox techniques did not weaken the quality of his work—indeed, they seemed to strengthen it. He would set the camera for the estimated distance, hold it above his head, and click the shutter. Nor did his unconventional style deny him positive recognition from his peers. In 1976, he was honored by the National Press Photographers Association with the Bert Williams Award.

Alone and aging, Bram slowly deteriorated until August 27, 1980, while he was brought down by an infection that ravaged his frail frame. Police found him ill in the doorway of a local business and took him to DePaul Hospital. Less than two weeks later he was moved to his final home at the Cheyenne Health Care Center.

More fortunate than many photographers, Bram reaped public praise in his declining years, thanks to his friend Margaret Laybourn, a long-time Cheyenne resident. She rescued more than 44,000 film and glass-plate negatives from the chaos of his photo lab and encouraged Bram to donate the mass of materials to the Wyoming State Museum. Volunteers subsequently sorted and arranged his pictorial treasury into a permanent collection depicting Cheyenne's past.

Although age and health halted his favorite hobbies of fishing, hiking, bicycling, and boomerang throwing, Bram continued to find joy in poetry and prose. Friends recall Bram reciting a passage from William Cullen Bryant's poem "Thanatopsis": "…approach thy grave, like one who wraps the drapery of his couch about him, and lies down to pleasant dreams."

Those sweet reveries came to Francis Brammar on April 19, 1986, four days before his eighty-sixth birthday.

❧ SOURCES CITED ❧ To know Brammar one must see his pictures. There is no better place for that than the Wyoming State Museum, where visitors may request a viewing. His collection was displayed there in 1984 and described in a commemorative brochure entitled *A Celebration of 50 Years of Cheyenne History through the Photos of Francis Brammar.*

It also is helpful to talk to some of those who knew him best. I interviewed such Cheyenne folks as Red Kelso on December 5, 1994 and January 15, 1995; Margaret Laybourn on January 11, 1995; and newspaper associate Kirk Knox on January 13, 1995.

An article by Bernard Horton shed light on his friendship with the eccentric photographer: "Bram has 'gone fishing'," *Sunday Eagle-Tribune*, Cheyenne, April 17, 1986. I found other details in public records, such as an undated Superintendent's Card, Laramie County School District No. 1, Cheyenne, Wyoming; the *Cheyenne City Directory* (Salt Lake City: R.I. Polk & Co. for 1918, 1926, 1928, 1929–30); "Action for Divorce," *Sydia Brammar, Plaintiff v. Ritner G. Brammar, Defendant*, Docket No. 178-145, Laramie County First District Court, Cheyenne, Wyoming, filed August 18, 1929; and Brammar's student records at the University of Wyoming, Laramie, as obtained via a telephone interview with Reba Macon on December 7, 1994.

Lastly, "Graveside Rites Tuesday for Francis Brammar," as published in the *Wyoming State Tribune*, Cheyenne, WY, on April 21, 1986, best describes his death and summarizes his life.

This chapter first appeared, in a slightly different form, in the *Casper Star-Tribune*, August 17, 1997.

CHAPTER 36

JOHN AND LILLIE SHANGRAU

MUSEUM COLLECTION HONORS NATIVE AMERICANS

THE BUCKSKINNED ARMY scout followed the two chilled Indian men into the tipi where a small rock-rimmed fire welcomed its guests.

Minutes seemed to pass. Only the moan of the cruel wind and the strained, irregular breathing at the edge of the darkness broke the silence. Then, near the bright coals in the center of the small group, one of the men slowly addressed his ailing host, Big Foot, chief of the Miniconjou Sioux. "The soldiers," he said, "want our guns, but …. Whatever you say, we will do."

The old man, racked with pneumonia, lay wrapped in a thick bison robe. "This is the third time they are going to take the guns away from me," he gasped, "but I will tell you, give them some of the bad guns, but keep the good ones."

Quietly the scout John Shangrau spoke from the shadows. "You better give up the guns. If you give the guns, you can get guns again … but if you lose a man you cannot replace him."

"No," Big Foot said firmly. "We will keep the good guns."

And so they kept the best weapons but lost their lives that bitter morn, December 29, 1890, on the banks of Wounded Knee Creek in what is now South Dakota.

As whites and Indians mingled on the American frontier, those who chose to mix their blood perhaps were less likely to spill it—or perhaps not. In 1820, French trapper-trader Julien Shangrau and an unidentified Indian woman had a child who bore the father's name, which was sometimes spelled Shangreaux. Most called the son Jules.

Thirty years later, young Jules was running a freight business from LaPorte, Colorado. Like his father, Jules wed an Indian, but she and their two children died of the white man's disease—smallpox. He later moved to Fort Laramie in Wyoming where he married Mary Smoke, daughter of Old Smoke, the famed Oglala Sioux chief. There Mary gave birth to John, the first of four sons.

After Jules died, twelve-year-old John took over his father's business, freighting with oxen between Fort Laramie on Wyoming's eastern border and Fort Kearny in central Nebraska. During the United States Army's 1876 Indian campaign John and his brother Louis joined a party of scouts headed to Fort Robinson in northwestern Nebraska, where they joined Brigadier General George Crook's command. The next few years must have severely tested the loyalties of John and those who shared his French and Indian background. For the white man's pay, they fought their Sioux and Cheyenne brothers whose homes hugged the hills along the waters of the Big Horn, Powder, and Yellowstone Rivers. At the same time, they waged a near-futile battle as advocates for the fair treatment of their foes.

At the close of the Indian Wars in May 1886, John married Mary Black Eyes, a Sioux who bore him three children. But when the mother and offspring died of an unrecorded disease, John returned to the army and served the next four years as chief of scouts under Brigadier General Thomas H. Ruger. About a week after the slaughter of the Sioux at Wounded Knee, the military reassigned John to escort some twenty more Indian captives to Chicago from their confinement at Fort Sheridan.

Finally, with his army work at an end, John joined the Wild West Show of his friend William "Buffalo Bill" Cody. While traveling Europe as the troupe's "Scout, Guide, and Interpreter, In Charge of Hostile Indians," John met nineteen-year-old Lillie Orr of Liverpool, England. Following a brief courtship, they wed in Glasgow, Scotland, on January 4, 1892. Ten months later, John brought his bride to America where she gave birth to their first child, Eleanore. During the next five years, they toured together with the Wild West Show and, over time, added nine more children to their family.

Around 1897 the Shangraus moved to Allen, South Dakota, where Lillie managed their store and post office while John traded at

John and Lillie Shangrau pose for their portrait amidst the flowers and greenery of a conservatory in London, England. Although its exact date is not recorded, this photo was taken between 1891, when they met in Lillie's hometown of Liverpool, and 1897, when John left "Buffalo Bill" Cody's Wild West Show and the couple moved to South Dakota. (Wyoming State Archives)

Indian reservations on both sides of the South Dakota–Nebraska line. The following year the family settled in Cody, Nebraska.

Assured by the Shangraus' success, Lillie's parents, her brother William, and sister Margaret left England in 1899 to join Lillie and her husband in the United States. Their move to the high plains must have been a culture shock: Lillie's father David Orr declared, upon seeing Cody for the first time, that it could not possibly be their destination. In fact, the former sea captain set sail on the surrounding sea of grass in search of the real city of Cody. Lillie's mother Eleanor simply sat down and cried. Despite the mental trauma, the Orrs decided to stay and homestead land north of town, near what is now known as Orr Lake. As the family prospered, William bought a two-story structure made of crude cottonwood planks. He later turned it over to Lillie, who managed a mercantile business in what became known as the Shangreaux Building. That is where the rest of the story took place.

In the late 1870s, civilians had contracted with the government's Bureau of Indian Affairs to establish trading posts on western reservations and Indian agencies. Many of these civilians were simply relatives of Indian agents or politicians, but John defied that stereotype. Not only was his mother from a prominent Sioux family, but he had earned the Indians' trust because of his empathy towards them when he worked as a military scout and manager of Buffalo Bill's cast. He also spoke the language of the Sioux who came to trade in his store, where merchandise such as knives, beads, pipes, tobacco, and furs could either be bartered or purchased with the white man's currency. Having little money, the Indians traded the items the Shangraus admired most: original, jewel-like art made of brightly colored beads and quills.

By the time John died at his ranch home northwest of Cody, Nebraska, on June 1, 1926, he had amassed nearly two hundred artifacts, including items representing all the Northern Plains tribes: beaded horse moccasins, a Grass Dance quirt, pipe bags, and dozens of others. The collection remained in Lillie's care until she too passed away on July 31, 1941. To protect that trove and celebrate the memory of their parents, the Shangrau children generously donated that part of their inheritance to the Wyoming State Museum.

And so John, who failed to save his people at Wounded Knee, left a legacy on their behalf that transcends their deaths. Thanks, too, to his love of beauty and Lillie's sense of history, visitors from around the world continue to be intrigued, instructed, and entertained by the Shangreaux Collection.

❖ SOURCES CITED ❖ The Wyoming State Museum, where one can view samples of the magnificent John and Lillie Shangrau Collection, is the place to start for those curious about their lives. I also learned much from members of his family: Lori Shangreaux of Pierre, South Dakota, on January 11, 1994; John Shangreaux of Las Cruces, New Mexico, on August 19 and 31, 1994; and Francis Shangreaux of Pine Ridge, South Dakota, on numerous occasions since 1994.

One of the more interesting interviews done with Shangrau, however, was accomplished by one of his contemporaries, Eli Ricker, who recorded details of that talk in what are known as the *Ricker Diaries*. Although the originals are on file at the Nebraska State Historical Society in Lincoln, a microfilmed copy is available to researchers at the Wyoming State Archives.

An ancillary source for details about the massacre is Dee Brown's *Bury My Heart at Wounded Knee* (New York: Holt, Rinehart & Winston, 1991).

This chapter first appeared, in a slightly different form, in the *Casper Star-Tribune*, September 7, 1997.

CHAPTER 37

"BIG NOSE" GEORGE PARROTT

FOUR TIMES A LOSER

EVEN OL' JUDGE Charles Lynch—from whom "lynch law" takes its name—might have blanched at "Big Nose" George Parrott's fate. Not once, but four times, the bad man stretched the string before a physician deemed him dead.

Although he first gained infamy as a horse thief, Parrott took his last steps on his path toward the land of the damned on August 17, 1878, on the tracks some three miles west of Medicine Bow in south-central Wyoming. There he and his gang pried the rail loose, aiming to stop and rob the train. An alert section boss saw the break as he walked the track, however, and called the law.

But when Carbon County Deputy Sheriffs Robert Widdowfield and Henry H. "Tip" Vincent found their prey holed up near Elk Mountain, the robbers struck first from their trap. Widdowfield fell with a slug in the back of his head. Vincent fired back, but with wounds in his chest and legs, he, too, died.

Almost two years passed before authorities finally caught Parrott after the drunken outlaw bragged of the killings one night in a Miles City, Montana, bar. As Carbon County Sheriff James Rankin escorted the murderer back by train to Wyoming, a mob at the town of Carbon snatched the prisoner, noosed his neck, and hauled him high before the choking man saved himself by confessing his crimes. Their work done, the vigilantes gave him back to the lawman, who took him on to Rawlins, the county seat.

In September 1880, following the felon's conviction for first-degree murder, a judge sentenced Parrott to be hanged the following April. But that spring, a little more than a week before the law

"Big Nose" George Parrott was described at the time of his death by some contemporaries as about thirty-five years old, five feet ten inches tall, and of "a rather spare" build. The black-haired bandit weighed about 160 pounds and sometimes wore a beard. In fact, one reporter said Parrott was "really not as bad a looking fellow as one would expect." (Wyoming State Archives)

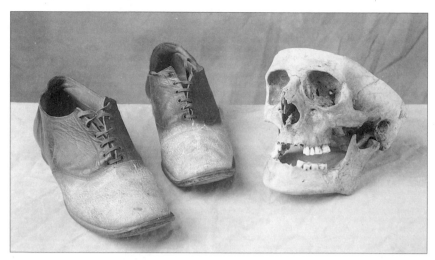

Shoes made from George Parrott's skin gained great attention for Dr. John E. Osborne, especially when he wore them to dances. "I instructed the shoemaker to keep the nipples on the skin," claimed Osborne, "to prove that the skin was that of a human. But he did not follow my instructions." (Craig Pindell, Carbon County Museum)

could dress him in a hemp tie, Parrott cut his way from his cell and tried to flee. Although he was stopped by jailer Robert Rankin and his wife, Rosa, an angry mob heard of his near-flight, stormed the jail, and dragged Parrott into the street. Near the railroad tracks, one in that group tossed a half-inch rope over the arm of a telegraph pole, while others shackled his feet and bound his hands behind his back. But they had not tested the rope, and it broke under his great weight when they tugged him into the air. In confusion, with the noose still around his neck, Parrott leaped from the ground and raced up a ladder leaning on the pole before a vigilante again grabbed the rope trailing over the telegraph's crossbar. Then after a bystander tightened the rope, someone else knocked the ladder from Parrott's feet. Gasping while grasping for the hemp, Parrot soon dropped his hands and his body swung free as his head fell to one side.

When Dr. John E. Osborne came on the scene, he had the body lowered so that he could verify Parrott was dead. The crowd, however, apparently still was not finished, so once again, the vigilantes hauled

Parrott high, and there he hung until the next day. Only then did they cut his body down for Osborne to take to his office where, first, he cast a plaster mask of the dead man's face. From Parrott's chest, the doctor later cut a piece of skin from which a cobbler made a pair of two-toned shoes. Some say Osborne subsequently wore those distinctive oxfords while accepting his oath as Wyoming's governor (his term was January 2, 1893–January 7, 1895). Still others claim that in 1896 he marched on those same soles through the halls of the United States Congress as Wyoming's representative. The doctor also trimmed his medicine bag with scraps from Parrott's hide and gave the outlaw's skull to his friend Dr. Lillian Heath, Wyoming's first woman physician (see chapter 27: "In the Hands of a Healer"). Dr. Heath used it as a flowerpot and pin dish as well as a doorstop.

While the power of the press helped burn the outlaw's name onto the pages of Western history, few gave a thought to the whereabouts of his remains. Certainly no relative ever appeared to claim them. Sixty-nine years after the lynching, builders laying the foundation of a store in Rawlins dug up a sealed whisky barrel. Stuffed inside they found what remained of Parrott's skeleton, a grisly memento of a doctor's curiosity and a big-nosed bandit's soul gone to hell.

❧ SOURCES CITED ❧ Perhaps the most macabre artifacts related to this story are "Big Nose" George's must-see skull as well as the handsome two-tone shoes made from his skin. Both are displayed at the Carbon County Museum in Rawlins, Wyoming.

Details of his life—or rather, what few details may be trusted—are best summarized in the following sources: Bennett R. Peace's "No Grave for Big Nose George," *The West* (Vol. 10, No. 6), May 1967; Daloney Otis Collins's "Skin Game in Old Wyoming," *Denver Post Empire Magazine,* November 17, 1974; Bill Bragg's "Sorting Curry from Currie, Big Nose from Flat Nose," *Casper Star-Tribune,* March 30, 1975; and Candy Moulton's "A Hard Way to Die," *Wyoming Weekend,* no date.

This chapter first appeared, in a slightly different form, in the *Casper Star-Tribune,* October 12, 1997.

CHAPTER 38

PONY EXPRESS RIDERS

MARE MAIL

APRIL 3, 1860. The bay mare's hooves spun a cloud of dust as well-wishers tried to pluck souvenir hairs from her mane and tail. But her rider, lean, young Johnny Fry, soon learned that their history-making mission would have to wait a few hours. Leaving the raucous crowd and blaring band, he spurred his mount back to the safe haven of the stables.

Finally, at 7:15 that evening, the brightly painted, brass-trimmed locomotive carrying the westbound mail roared into the river town of St. Joseph, Missouri, spewing a plume of smoke that left gray ash in its wake. The roar of a cannon signaled the ferry *Ebenezer* to dock and prepare to carry Fry, in his embroidered, silver-trimmed costume, and his steed Sylph to Elwood on the Kansas side of the Missouri River. The big gun's report also fetched the lad at a gallop back through the tumult to St. Joseph's Pony Express office where an attendant draped a leather *mochila* over the lightweight, shell-like saddle on his horse. Eighty-five pieces of correspondence and a special edition of the St. Joseph *Daily Gazette* filled the four pouches, each secured with a small brass padlock.

At the appointed time, Mayor M. Jeff Thompson slapped the filly's flank and sent her and her passenger bounding down the hill and onto the waiting boat. Once across the river, Fry and subsequent riders braved fierce elements and physical hardships as they relayed the mail across the American frontier. Two hundred and thirty-nine hours would pass before the last jockey on that route reached Sacramento, California, nearly two thousand miles west.

But the Pony Express did not rest. At about 2:45 A.M. the next day, Billy Hamilton left Sacramento with the eastbound mail. The last man on his team reached St. Joe ten days later. Although the service began with riders leaving once a week, twice a week soon became the norm.

More than 180 daring riders would serve the Pony Express over the next eighteen months. To recruit them, the outfit's owners—William H. Russell, Alexander Majors, and William B. Waddell—placed an ad in newspapers across the United States: "WANTED—Young, skinny, wiry fellows not over 18. Must be expert riders willing to risk death daily. Orphans preferred. Wages $25 per week." Most of those selected received calf-bound Bibles and Colt pistols. They also pledged to "use no profane language…drink no intoxicating liquors… [and] not quarrel or fight with any other employee of the firm."

During each Missouri-to-California trip, some twenty-five daring youths each spent eight to ten hours in the saddle. Each rode seventy-five to a hundred miles, stopping to change horses every ten to fifteen miles at a Pony Express stop. Manned by a total staff of about four hundred, the stations dotted the route across the West.

Pony Express clerks at first charged five dollars a half-ounce for messages passing through their system. They reduced that amount to one dollar, however, after customers began writing their notes on tissue-like paper, which they rolled pencil-thin and wrapped protectively in oiled silk.

Despite the hazards of weather, terrain, Indians, and outlaws, Pony Express riders such as William "Buffalo Bill" Cody (see chapter 29: "The Legends and Life of an American Legend") and "Pony Bob" Haslam performed awesome feats. Over three hundred runs were made each way, totaling some 65,000 miles. Each such trip averaged ten days at ten miles per hour. A total of 35,000 pieces of mail were delivered.

Miraculously, despite many staff casualties, only one mail pouch was ever lost. The Pony Express also set a delivery speed record that

A Pony Express station tender and his assistant drape a leather mochila *(Spanish for knapsack), its four pockets loaded with mail and mail parcels, over the shell-like saddle on the rider's fresh horse.* (Wyoming State Archives)

still seems incredible: a copy of President Abraham Lincoln's east coast inaugural address arrived at its California destination in seven days, seventeen hours.

The Pony Express served several other functions. It succeeded in promoting their stage and freight line while proving conclusively the year-round effectiveness of Russell, Majors, and Waddell's route, called the Central Overland. The October 24, 1861, completion of the transcontinental telegraph, however, signaled the end of pony mail, although sporadic deliveries continued for about a month more.

Although the Pony Express officially lasted only 570 days, the courage, endurance, and deeds of its employees still excite America's imagination.

❧ SOURCES CITED ❧ My July 3, 1995, telephone interview with Jackie Lewin, curator of the Pony Express National Memorial in St. Joseph,

Missouri, was very helpful in fleshing out this story. So, too, were the background publications she provided from the St. Joseph Museum: "Pony Express National Memorial Grand Opening Commemorative Program," April 3, 1993; "Pony Express Information Fact Sheet," St. Joseph, Missouri, no date; and "Pony Express National Memorial Fact Sheet," March 1994. Another, "The Pony Express Rides Again," April 3, 1993, came from the Pony Express National Memorial.

Valuable secondary sources included Fred Reinfeld's book *Pony Express* (Lincoln, NE: University of Nebraska Press, 1966) as well as the articles "The Pony Express Rider Hits the Trail 100 Years Ago Today," *Sunday Register*, Des Moines, IA, April 3, 1960; and James Patterson's "Pony Express!" in *Denver Post Empire Magazine*, February 23, 1975.

Additional information came from Kate B. Carter's *Riders of the Pony Express* (Salt Lake City: Central Co., Daughters of Utah Pioneers, 1947); L.C. Bishop's "Report on Pony Express Stations Across Wyoming," published by the Wyoming Pony Express Centennial Board, Cheyenne, December 5, 1959; and the Pony Express vertical/subject file at the Wyoming State Archives.

This chapter first appeared, in a slightly different form, in the *Casper Star-Tribune*, October 26, 1997.

CHAPTER 39

Edwin P. Taylor

CHEYENNE'S "TAYLOR-MADE" FIRE DEPARTMENT

ONE CAN STILL imagine that Sunday scene from hell on December 18, 1916. Long tongues of flame licked the late night sky over downtown Cheyenne as guests at the Inter-Ocean Hotel, trapped in their rooms, screamed for help. In desperation a thirty-year-old man leaped through a third-floor window. But instead of finding a net, he fell across a hot 2300-volt power line that curled and crisped his corpse like a strip of well-cooked bacon.

Before those coals cooled, the blaze would nearly raze the famous building while claiming more lives than any fire in the city's history before or since. Six lives were lost: Roy and Ethel White and their four sons, Francis, age seven; Donald, five; Guy, three; and nine-month-old Hubert. The Whites had stopped in Cheyenne on their way from the Iowa funeral of Roy's father to their home in California.

Later that same evening, another inferno several blocks south charred a Union Pacific coach shop and storeroom valued at more than $100,000. Investigators claimed "defective wiring" caused both fires.

Regrettably, Edwin "Ed" P. Taylor, who later wore the sleek leather hat shown in this chapter, knew similar horrors and losses during his thirty-seven years with the Cheyenne Fire Department. Taylor was born August 3, 1876, at Fort Sanders, near Laramie, Wyoming. He spent most of his childhood at such other military posts as Fort Laramie, Camp Carlin, and Fort D.A. Russell (now F.E. Warren Air Force Base) near Cheyenne, and at Fort Robinson near Crawford, Nebraska. Taylor first found work outside his home as an "inker" boy on an old Washington handpress at the *Boomerang*

This painted leather fireman's hat, circa 1930, usually saw duty on the Cheyenne Fire Department chief's head only at parades and similar special events. (Wyoming State Museum)

newspaper in Laramie. He also worked briefly in that city at a rolling mill before he moved to Cheyenne, where he became a volunteer member of the Pioneer Hook and Ladder Company No. 1 in April 1893. During this period, he apparently supported himself by returning to his journalistic roots and apprenticing at the *Cheyenne Daily Sun.* Later, with the *Cheyenne Daily Leader,* he learned to operate a complex Linotype machine before signing up for military service when the Spanish-American War broke out in 1898.

When that conflict ended the next year, the young man returned to his newspaper work and volunteer service with the fire department in Cheyenne. Local authorities there also gave him the extra duty of supervising the militia guard surrounding the Laramie County Courthouse during the November 20, 1903, hanging of the convicted murderer Tom Horn.

Thanks in part to his unflagging service as a volunteer fireman, Fire Chief Percy Hoyt appointed him as his "lieutenant." But Taylor held the position just six weeks, from May 1 to June 13, 1909,

Fire Chief Edwin P. Taylor, right, and an unidentified colleague pose in a Cheyenne Fire Department buggy, circa 1915, in front of the old Pioneer Fire Headquarters on Eddy Street, now Pioneer Avenue. (Wyoming State Archive)

when he resigned. Taylor wrote later he had crossed swords with Hoyt "because of politics."

Hoyt, a wealthy philanthropist, had professionalized his department by paying his firemen's salaries and buying most of its equipment himself. But the fiery fire chief also tangled with the city's administration. In fact, a year and a half later, on January 1, 1911, Hoyt quit, piqued with Mayor Lawrence R. Bresnahan over his strained relations with Taylor and other matters. Hoyt took back most of the items he purchased for the department and left the city. The mayor reappointed Taylor to the fire department on February 16, made him acting chief on March 8, then appointed him fire chief on April 16, 1912.

During the company's next six years under Taylor's leadership, city officials bought new fire equipment. Thus, for the first time since Cheyenne had formed its initial company of firefighters in 1867, it had motorized, self-sufficient firefighting capabilities worthy of its capital city status.

Thanks as much to the encouragement of organized labor as to Taylor's administrative skills, Governor John B. Kendrick appointed him Wyoming's first commissioner of labor and statistics, a job he held from the time he resigned as fire chief on March 1, 1917 until July 15, 1918. Bitten hard by the political bug, he soon turned his attentions to local politics and succeeded on January 5, 1920, in becoming Cheyenne's twenty-sixth mayor. At the end of his second consecutive term, Taylor yielded to his successor, Charles W. Riner, who reappointed him as fire chief, a job he held until his retirement on New Year's Day sixteen years later.

Taylor died at age eighty-one on January 31, 1958, while being treated in the DePaul Hospital at Cheyenne. Following local Catholic services, his wife Luna buried him at the Arlington National Cemetery in Virginia.

❧ SOURCES CITED ❧ The fire chief's helmet that Ed Taylor wore when he held that position during 1911–16 and 1926–42 may be inspected, along with its accession papers, at the Wyoming State Museum.

I learned much about Taylor's accomplishments during a September 30, 1997, interview in Cheyenne with Bill Allen, himself a former firefighter and local fire department member.

Additional facts about that department can be obtained from the chapter titled "History—Cheyenne Fire Department," in *History of Cheyenne, Wyoming, Laramie County*, Sharon Lass Field, ed., Vol. 2 (Cheyenne, WY: Curtis Media Corp., 1989).

This chapter first appeared, in a slightly different form, in the *Casper Star-Tribune*, November 9, 1997.

CHAPTER 40

Walt Lambertsen

"GENTLEMEN, START YOUR BUGS"

By nine in the morning—still two and a half hours before start time for the round-trip auto race from Rock Springs to Pinedale, Wyoming—hundreds of spectators had already gathered. They lined the route from the air-mail landing field at Rock Springs to far north of town. Grease-stained drivers and mechanics in oil-soaked coveralls took advantage of that free time to air their tires and tune their carbs.

But those last idle hours on July 4, 1922, masked many prior months of prep work. To shape their "bugs" into sleek, scarab-like shells, the teams had cut, bent, and welded sheet-steel into round aft sections that would slip more smoothly through the air. Those same crews schemed in still more ways to improve their odds. Twenty-four-year-old Walt Lambertsen, who worked for the Lincoln Highway Garage in Rawlins, put a special sump into the cockpit of his Detroit-made Essex so that Frank Keefe, his ride-along grease monkey, might pump oil from it to top off the engine's reservoir. The driver knew, too, that air-filled tires posed risks. So the night before the race, he and Keefe pulled the tubes, vulcanizing each to help guard against the burrs and sharp stones lining the rough, unpaved trail.

Their rivals, it seems, did not plan so well. For a host of reasons, only three of fourteen entries found their way to the line that day. H. A. Collison, an air-mail pilot driving a Ford, pulled the number-one position for the staggered start.

Finally, with the clock ticked down to 11:23:30, a race official stepped forward and shouted "Go!" As onlookers plugged their ears

This Essex car, driven by Walt Lambertsen (at the wheel) with his mechanic Frank Keefe, won the July 4, 1922, round-trip Rock Springs–Pinedale auto race. They averaged more than fifty miles per hour over the 202 miles in only four hours, six minutes, and thirty seconds. (Carbon County Museum)

amidst grinding gears, Collison's car roared north across Bad Land Hills toward its first stop at the Eden post office. The thick treads on his wheels spun a great grey cloud that left a coat of fine dust on all in its wake. Precisely ten minutes later, Lander's own "Red" Seebright and his rebuilt Essex shot from the line. Finally, as the third and last car—Lambertsen's pine-tree green machine—sped away at 11:43:30 and churned out of sight, the crowd eased back to Rock Springs where the snap and bang of firecrackers welcomed their return.

Back in town, the kids got set to sprint North and South Front Streets for prizes. Meanwhile, at 11:51, eighteen miles to the northwest, Collison drove past the woodshed at the Wells place where shearers clipped their sheep.

Seebright's number-two car, slowed by an ailing engine, limped into that site a full fifteen minutes later. It broke a piston soon thereafter and quit the race.

Overtaking Seebright, Lambertsen and Keefe steamed past his car which sat in shambles by the side of the road. Then through

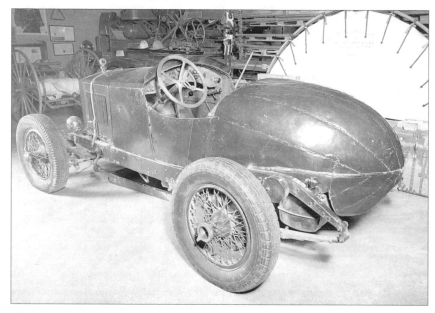

Walt Lambertsen's race car, which he drove for pleasure as well as profit, was painted pine-tree green when he raced the Essex in 1922. His eldest son Keith later repainted the car maroon. (Carbon County Museum)

sand and sage they chugged on to Wells, arriving there at 12:06, barely five minutes off the front-runner's time. After passing Eden fifteen minutes later, the surviving Essex dashed on to Farson only four miles further north. Led by snow-capped peaks to the west, the hard-driving crew crossed Sandy Creek and cut through Sublette's Flats toward the turn-pole at Pinedale.

In the meantime, while bouncing over the bridge at Boulder Creek, Collison had snapped the frame of his car. As he splinted the side bar with wire and a wood rail, Lambertsen and Keefe caught up and slid to a near halt. To avoid the same plight, Lambertsen eased his tires across the gap between the road and the bridge boards, then slowly spanned the stream. After twelve more miles, he and Keefe screeched to a stop at 1:43:30 in Pinedale, on the west flank of the Wind River Range. A mere two and a half minutes later, with a full load of fresh water and gas, Lambertsen turned his metal mount and headed for home.

Retracing their tracks to Farson, Lambertsen and Keefe continued through Eden and, again, across the broad Great Divide Basin before arriving in Rock Springs at exactly 3:50. Their elapsed time that day? Four hours, six minutes, and thirty seconds, including four stops that totaled eight minutes.

For their first-place finish, Lambertsen and Keefe pocketed five hundred dollars, while Collison, who gimped back to town in second place with his fractured frame, earned two hundred. And poor Seebright, who failed to finish, took home a hundred dollars in one of the great road races to grace southwest Wyoming. Old-timers there claim only the gas-guzzlers that growled through Rock Springs during the epic 1908 auto race from New York to Paris caused more fuss.

❧ SOURCES CITED ❧ After inspecting Walt Lambertsen's race car at the Carbon County Museum—which also has a special photo display devoted to it and the July 4, 1922 race—I talked with Keith Lambertsen in Rawlins by phone on September 23 and November 5, 1997, to learn more about his father's life and experiences with automobiles. The old auto mechanic-racer's obituary, "Walter Morris Lambertsen," appeared in the *Rawlins Daily Times*, August 6, 1985.

Several thrilling accounts of the famed race itself can be found in the following newspaper articles: "The Glorious Fourth Will Be Appropriately Celebrated in City," *Rock Springs Rocket*, June 30, 1922; "The Glorious Forth Celebration Proves Great Success in the City," *Rock Springs Rocket*, July 6, 1922; "Car Makes Good Time," *Pinedale Roundup*, July 7, 1922; "Winner of the Rock Springs-Pinedale Auto Race July 4th;" *Rawlins Republican*, July 13, 1922; and "Snap Shots at Home News," *Wyoming State Journal*, Lander, Wyoming, July 14, 1922.

This chapter first appeared, in a slightly different form, in the *Casper Star-Tribune*, November 23, 1997.

CHAPTER 41

ROSE ECOFFEY

"PRINCESS BLUE WATER," CHAMPION FOR HER PEOPLE

"THE ROYAL PARTY," famed showman William F. "Buffalo Bill" Cody is quoted as saying in a 1993 *Old West* article, "cottoned greatly to John Nelson's half-breed papoose." The royals did, that is, until the snip stubbornly refused to curtsy or kiss Queen Victoria's hand. The child reasoned—she said later—that when she met America's president, he did not demand such courtesies. Why should a mere queen?

Who was this precocious imp who snubbed the English monarch? "Princess Blue Water" was chosen as Rose Nelson's stage name, some say, by "Buffalo Bill" to honor her crossing of the Atlantic as a performer with his Wild West Show.

Rosie, with her black eyes and skin the hue of rich soil, found life March 15, 1880, on the Pine Ridge Reservation, thanks to the match of a coarse mountain man and an Oglala Lakota Sioux maid. There, near Craven Creek in south-central South Dakota, she and her parents shared a tipi with her siblings John Jr., Julia, Tom, and Jim.

During 1887 and 1888, Cody hired Rosie's father, John Young Nelson, as an interpreter and sharpshooter for his traveling troupe. Nelson's wife, Jennie Lone Wolf—daughter of Chief Smoke and sister of Chief Red Cloud—and their children also toured the United States and England on that trip. Annie Oakley, also with Cody's group, spanked the child's bottom on more than a few occasions because of her behavior.

Soon after the family returned to America, Dr. "Colonel" Frank Powell, a partner in the Wild West Show, took Rosie under his wing and sent her to the prestigious Franklin Institute in Philadelphia.

"Princess Blue Water" was the stage name of Rose Powell Nelson, who performed with Buffalo Bill's Wild West Show throughout the United States and England in 1887 and 1888. She poses here under the hand of her father, John Young Nelson, with (from left) her brothers, Jim and Tom; her mother, Jenny; sister, Julia, and her eldest brother, John Jr. (Wyoming State Archives)

There she gained a sound elementary education, as well as an understanding of art and music.

Back on the Pine Ridge Reservation, sixteen-year-old Rosie met Joseph Ecoffey, an educated Nebraska Sandhills rancher and grandson of one-time Fort Laramie post trader Joseph Bissonette. They wed on March 27, 1896, and had nine children: Louise, Frank, Ethel, Evelyn, Lenore, Edward, Lawrence, Stella, and Alvina. While the family lived on the reservation, President Theodore Roosevelt stopped at that federal site as part of an inspection visit during his second term (1905–09). At the gala staged in his honor, some claim that Rosie not only met America's twenty-sixth chief executive, she counted coup by waltzing with him.

Rosie launched her work in 1926 as an advocate for and defender of those Native Americans who most suffered those trying times. She also voluntarily took on leadership responsibilities not normally considered "woman's work." For many years Rosie led the Lakota delegation from Pine Ridge to the world-famous Frontier Days in Cheyenne. As her tribe's agent for their participation in that grand affair, she proved to be a tough negotiator by insisting the Frontier Days Committee pick up the tab for her group's travel, food, and lodging. She also demanded—and got—top daily wages for her people: three dollars and fifty cents for men (fourteen years and older) and three dollars for women. Children earned half pay, plus all the coins they could collect from audiences.

Thanks to Rosie's political clout, powerful friends, and her effective advocacy as a lay tribal lawyer, Oglala Lakota elders appointed her to the National Council of Indians. Her success in that role led to her 1940 selection as the first woman to serve as a judge on a Native American tribal court. In recognition of such public service, President John F. Kennedy invited Rosie, a staunch Democrat and precinct chairwoman at Pine Ridge, to attend his 1961 inauguration in Washington, D.C.

Inevitably, however, her advancing years and poor health kept her close to home. When the Frontier Days Board of Directors brought her to a ceremony in Cheyenne on December 27, 1965, they honored her fifty years of "loyal and diligent service" with a bronze plaque and a silver lifetime pass to "The Daddy of 'Em All."

Finally, ninety-two winters took their toll. Rosie died at 6:45 the evening of Sunday, June 11, 1972, in the Good Samaritan Hospital at Gordon, Nebraska. Her family buried her in their plot in the Pine Ridge Reservation's cemetery.

Despite the great void left by her passing, Rosie's proudest legacy—her progeny—live on. Her 225 direct descendants at this writing include 37 grandchildren, 165 great-grandchildren, and 18 great, great-grandchildren.

⊱ SOURCES CITED ⊱ I gained most of the genealogical details for this story about Rose Nelson Ecoffey—aka Princess Blue

Rose Nelson Ecoffey admires her grandson Ed Ecoffey's traditional costume. Ed's great-grandmother made the beaded white buckskin jacket and leggings sixty-eight years earlier, in 1880, for his grandfather Joe. (Marirose Morris collection)

At the Frontier Days Old West Museum, the Princess Blue Water Exhibit honors Rose Powell Nelson Ecoffey for her years of loyal service to the famed Frontier Days celebration. (Craig D. Pindell, Cheyenne Frontier Days Old West Museum)

Water—and her family during a July 30, 1997, interview with her granddaughter Marirose Morris at her home in Cheyenne.

Additional facts came from a variety of secondary sources, such as William B. Secrest's "'Indian' John Nelson," *Old West*, November 30, 1993; Barbara E. Andre's "Marrying Squaw—Man Gets Trapped," *The West*, no date; Margaret Laybourn's "Princess Bluewater," *Senior Voice*, Ft. Collins, Colorado, June 1995; Betty Schroll's "The Legacy of Princess Blue Water," *Wyoming Catholic Register*, Cheyenne, Wyoming, July 1990; "Rose Powell Nelson," *The Shannon County News*, Pine Ridge Indian Reservation, Pine Ridge, South Dakota (Vol. 33, No. 178), June 16, 1972; "Where Do the Indians Come From?" *Denver Post Empire Magazine*, July 21, 1968; and Pat Stuart's "Princess Blue Water Dead at 92," *Cheyenne Sunday Tribune-Eagle*, June 18, 1972.

This chapter first appeared, in a slightly different form, in the *Casper Star-Tribune*, September 14, 1997.

CHAPTER 42

GOVERNOR MIKE SULLIVAN

A CHAT WITH A HAT

RETURNING FROM THE vault with a box in her white-gloved hands, the young woman entered the small, well-lit room. She placed the parcel on the table in front of the reporter and briefly instructed him as to its care. Then she turned and left.

In silence, the scribe gazed at the grey cardboard cube. Then, he, too, donned white cotton mitts and lifted its lid. Inside, he found the object of his quest: the torn, sweat-stained, beige hat once worn on Wyoming's past head of state: Governor Mike Sullivan. Removing it with care, the newsman held the artifact close and eyed it with quiet admiration. "You've seen some tough times, haven't you?" he asked with a smile.

"Yup, a few," yawned the Stetson, still fresh from its long nap. "I recall my harsh youth when I was cut, bent, and blocked into the 'Open Road' style of hat so prized by men like Mike. But I've had good times, too. Like when I came north from Texas to join kin brought here more than a century ago. In fact, I'm sure you've seen perhaps the best known of my forebears...the hat in the hand of the cowpoke who rides the bronc on all Wyoming car tags.

"Like *it*," continued the fine felt voice from the deep-creased crown, "I linked up with a great guy—my best friend, Mike Sullivan. We traveled together everywhere. For twenty-nine years I shielded him from sun, wind, rain, and snow. Then, with kindness, he retired me to the Wyoming State Museum Collection Center here in Cheyenne."

"So, how did you and the Governor make a match?"

"We met, I believe, around 1968. Harry Yesness introduced us at his men's store in Casper where Mike worked as an attorney. What a man! We matched up right off, you might say. My size seven-and-a-half made the perfect mate for his follicularly impaired pate."

"Tell me about it."

"Well, I learned right quick that there are no surprises with Mike. He's honest, true, and a friend indeed to those in need. And he don't cut slack for those who won't pull their weight. Best of all, he takes you as you are, even if, as in my case, you're somewhat the worse for wear."

Continuing, the writer asked, "So tell me about his past."

"That's easy," said the cowboy cap. "Born September 22, 1939, in Omaha, Nebraska, to J.B. and Margaret Hamilton Sullivan. Mike, you see, grew up in Douglas, Wyoming, where he graduated in 1957 from Converse County High School. Like his folks, he went to the University of Wyoming, where he gained a Bachelor of Science four years later in petroleum engineering. That's just about the time he married Jane Metzler with whom he raised three children: Michelle, Patrick, and Theresa.

"But first, in 1964, he earned his *Juris Doctor* sheepskin, with honors, then practiced law in Casper, specializing in trial work. And following his most recent stint as U.S. ambassador to Ireland, he's back in Casper again, this time as special counsel for the firm Rothgerber, Johnson & Lyons LLP. And he loves to fish, jog, and swat golf and tennis balls. Still does. In fact, those outings caused most of my scars.

"But the worst wear and tear of my life came after he tossed me into the political ring and hit the campaign trail."

"Yes," said the journalist. "I understand his friend Charlie Crowe, who failed in his race against Cliff Hansen for the governor's job, warned: 'Don't wear that old hat!' Did that hurt you?"

"You bet, but Governor Mike sticks by his friends, no matter what. Oh, he took Charlie's words to heart, but we'd been pals so long that, when he made his rounds of all those 'teas' to grip and grin, he'd just forget until, the next thing he knew, he'd find me still perched atop that old familiar spot. And before long, he even said with pride that I was his 'signature.' Apparently it didn't hurt him

*Mike Sullivan, Wyoming's twenty-ninth governor, bought his famed Stetson in 1968
at Harry Yesness's men's shop in Casper.* (Wyoming State Archives)

too much to pair up with me because the voters chose him in their
1986 election to be Wyoming's twenty-ninth governor."

"But"—the reporter cut in again—"you almost cost him his reelection four years later, didn't you?"

"Some claim that's so," said the Stetson. "As I recall, things went
well until late 1988 when Mike and I rode 'round the field with
some duded-up dignitaries before Wyoming played at the Holiday
Bowl football game in San Diego. Then a guy named Bill Benson
from Cheyenne saw us from his seat in the stands. My poor condition, he claimed, caused him such shame that, upon his return

home he fired off a note to the *Casper Star-Tribune*'s editor. It was published November 29, chiding Mike's 'filthy, ratty hat.' That charge spurred a rash of replies from 'round the state—pro and con—that soon saw publication in that same newspaper. '*It's what's under Gov Suv's hat that's important*,' steamed the headline of Wanda Day's December 1 retort from Fort Washakie. Others blared back in boldface type that '*Guv, if you're representing me, lose your hat*'... '*An English derby or French beret ain't Wyoming*'... '*Western governors don't need movie star hats or ways.*' Chip and Susan Carlson of Cheyenne even proposed a fundraiser to 'Get Mike a Better Hat.'

"But the best scold, as I recall, came December 27 when Dr. Bob Carlson, a Casper College scholar, reminded all that 'the head upon which Sullivan's hat rests is that which governs, not the hat.'

"He's right, of course. But what's a king without a crown?"

⚭ SOURCES CITED ⚭ I've written few stories that were as much fun or as daunting as this one. Why? Well, first I had to interview the subject itself: the hat (artifact #995.3.2) at its home in the Wyoming State Museum. Then, of course, it was necessary to contact the man who knows it best: Mike Sullivan, former governor of Wyoming and United States ambassador to Ireland. The latter talk took place on October 30, 1997. I chatted, too, on November 4, 1997, with William Benson, who had found the hat such a poor representative of his state. Lastly, the following day, I interviewed by phone an unnamed technician at the Stetson Hat Company in Garland, Texas, who earns his living by making such chapeaus.

And to flesh out this tale I found most of what I needed in the letters-to-the-editor section of the *Casper Star-Tribune* for the period November 29 through December 29, 1988.

This chapter first appeared, in a slightly different form, in the *Casper Star-Tribune*, December 21, 1997.

CHAPTER 43

ADOLPH METZGER

THE FETTERMAN FIGHT: THE MAKING OF A MYTH

THE BUGLE'S MOUTHPIECE is missing, and its battered bell and body—smashed flat as a fritter—have been mute for nearly a century and a half. That herald's last call, however, rings so loud and clear in America's mythology that some think they still can hear the soldier's cry for help.

That tarnished horn, they say, belonged to Adolph Metzger, a Company C bugler with the United States Army's Second Cavalry at Fort Phil Kearny, Wyoming Territory. But when we look into his past and tales of the 1866 Fetterman Fight in which he is believed to have died, we find that the more we learn, the less we know.

Take that bugle, for example. More than a few old-timers claim in good faith that Metzger bashed a few brains with its brass before Indians feathered his body with their arrows. John Gutherie, one of Metzger's Company C mates, had some doubts. When he went to help recover the bodies that same day, he reported that "Metzer [sic] ... we never found, It was thought that Col. Fetterman sent him to the fort for reinforcement and he was cut off by the Indians."

But if either or both of those accounts are false, may we find truth on the plaque of the Fetterman Monument dedicated July 3, 1908?

> On this field on the 21st day of December 1866, three com-missioned officers and **seventy-six privates** of the 18th U.S. Infantry and of the 2nd U.S. Cavalry, and **four civilians,** under the command of Captain Brevet-Lieutenant Colonel William J. Fetterman [18th Infantry] were killed by an over-whelming force of **Sioux** under the command of Red Cloud. There were **no survivors** [author's emphases].

No, the truth eludes us. Accounts vary widely in several respects.

First, according to post-battle Army reports, the seventy-eight troops who died that day included fifty-five privates, three officers, two civilians, eight sergeants, ten corporals, one bugler (Metzger), one "artificer" (skilled craftsman), and one "unassigned recruit."

Second, Army witnesses testified, only two civilians died that cold, grey day: James S. Wheatley and Isaac Fisher.

Third, Sioux participants acknowledged that about one hundred fifty Cheyenne and sixty Arapaho had joined their carefully planned maneuver.

And fourth, not only did most of the Indians survive that blood rout, but Fort Phil Kearny's commander Colonel Henry B. Carrington told his superiors that at least nine Indian ponies and eleven military horses survived the fight, including "Dapple Dave," a mount believed to be from Metzger's unit. He also reported that the Indians numbered nearly 3,000 and "lost beyond all precedent." The consensus now is that 1,500 to 2,000 Indian participants may be more accurate. Doubt still reigns as to Indian casualties. Although the army claimed it slew nearly as many as it lost in the "massacre," the Sioux insisted only eight of their men lost their lives on the battleground. Of about fifty injured, they said twenty-two later died of their wounds.

Perhaps the most intriguing tale deals with the alleged suicides of Captain Frederick H. Brown, Company E, Eighteenth Infantry, and Fetterman himself. Legend has them shooting guns at each other's temples to avoid capture and torture. However, Assistant Surgeon Samuel M. Horton, who conducted their autopsies, stated:

Col. Fetterman's body showed his thorax to have been cut crosswise with a knife, deep into the viscera; his throat and entire neck were cut to the cervical spine, all around. I believe that mutilation caused his death.

This seems to jibe with Sioux Chief American Horse's account that he "ran his horse at full speed directly on to Col. Fetterman knocking him down ... then jumped down upon him and killed the

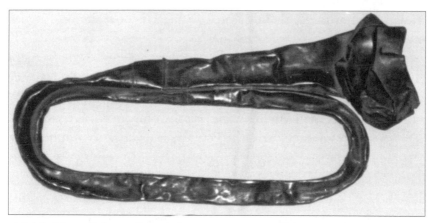

Adolph Metzger's last call for help, some say, may still be trapped deep inside the crushed, tarnished bell and body of this U.S. Army bugle. (Jim Gatchell Memorial Museum, Buffalo, Wyoming)

colonel with...[a] knife." Only Brown's temple, said Doctor Horton, showed signs of a fatal, self-inflicted pistol shot.

So, who and what are we to believe? Although the Indians won the fight that day, they lost the war against a foe who bought ink by the barrel, as evidenced by the voluminous histories they wrote about that battle. "Metzger's" broken bugle remains a metaphor not only for those who blindly led their men like hare into that snare, but those who set the trap. It memorializes, too, those souls—on both sides—who followed and fell in the line of duty.

❧ SOURCES CITED ❧ Ironically, I know of no more eloquent voice for those soldiers and Indians who died in the Fetterman Fight than that of Metzger's bugle itself, although some experts question whether it was, in fact, present at the battle. Regardless, one can hear the tale it tells—as I did on December 5, 1997—by visiting the Jim Gatchell Memorial Museum of the West in Buffalo, Wyoming.

Though some doubt its credentials, both the bugle and the Fetterman monument, which I last visited on July 23, 1997, still commemorate one of the most important battles between the military and Indians. To better understand the significance of that conflict, I spoke by phone with Bob Wilson, assistant superintendent and curator at the Fort Phil Kearny State Historic Site on August 25, 1997.

Perhaps the best-documented secondary sources on the subject include John Gutherie's recollections titled "Massacre Monument" (Washington, D.C., U.S. Home, Fort Phil Kearny, no date), on file at the Wyoming State Archives. He was a Company C, Second Cavalry veteran. Also useful were the Fetterman Fight Map produced by the Sheridan Press, Sheridan, Wyoming, dated December 21, 1985; Deanne Umbach Kardik's *Adolph Metzger, Portrait of Fort Phil Kearny* (Banner, Wyoming: Fort Phil Kearny–Bozeman Trail Association, 1993); and three articles: John D. McDermott's "Price of Arrogance: The Short & Controversial Life of William Judd Fetterman," "Wyoming Scrapbook: Documents Relating to the Fetterman Fight," and Elbert D. Belish's "American Horse: the Man Who Killed Fetterman," all in *Annals of Wyoming* (Vol. 63, No. 2), Spring 1991.

This chapter first appeared, in a slightly different form, in the *Casper Star-Tribune*, December 7, 1997.

CHAPTER 44

William Jefferson Hardin

WYOMING'S FIRST BLACK LEGISLATOR

At CHEYENNE'S OPERA House, the blaze in the fireplace snapped and cracked like a whip that winter, barely caging the chill in the drafty hall as Wyoming's Seventh Legislative Assembly met from January 10 through March 10, 1882. As the men warmed to their work that season, they repealed a law passed thirteen years earlier by the state's first legislative assembly: a law that banned interracial marriages.

That group included a proud, bronze-skinned gentleman with jet-black hair and eyes, who wore his 140 pounds slickly on his five-foot, ten-inch frame. As Wyoming's first black legislator, he probably felt joy, because the brave votes the majority joined in casting de-stigmatized his birth and legitimized his marriage.

Born in 1829 or 1830 in Russellville, Kentucky, the son of a free black mother and a white father, William Jefferson Hardin traveled a rough road to reach the lofty life he lived in Cheyenne.

Thanks to a fine early education by Shakers, he became a schoolteacher in Bowling Green. There, on June 15, 1850, he married Caroline Catherine Butcher, a woman close to his own age, of about twenty. Like her husband, Caroline and her fourteen siblings shared a mixed-blood heritage: their mother, Mary, was African-American, while Mr. Butcher's lineage was half American Indian and half German.

Although the cause of the Hardins' subsequent separation is not clear, history records that sometime after 1850, gold called William west to California. Not long after, Mrs. Butcher moved her offspring, including Caroline, to Canada, fearing they might be caught and sold as slaves in the United States.

William Jefferson Hardin, Wyoming's first black legislator, served in the Sixth and Seventh Legislative Assemblies from November 4, 1879 through December 31, 1884. (Wyoming State Archives)

William seems briefly to have rejoined his spouse in Ontario before continuing alone to Wisconsin and then on through Iowa and Nebraska before settling in Denver in 1863. In the Mile High City Hardin soon prospered as a barber, becoming a leader in the black community. In fact, the dynamic speaker became so well known in his fight for equal rights, black suffrage, and the integration of public schools that newspapers dubbed him the "Colored Orator of Denver." He proved so popular and effective that local Republican leaders chose him to represent them at their party's 1872 Territorial Convention. The following year, those same appreciative pols helped him land a job as a gold weigher and clerk with the Denver branch of the United States Mint. In 1873 he also wed Nellie Davidson, a white woman from New York, who worked locally as a milliner.

But soon thereafter Caroline burst on scene to shout "Bigamist!" and to tell all who would listen that she had not only wed Hardin in Kentucky, but in 1858 had borne him a daughter, Mary Elizabeth. Further, she charged that Hardin moved from Omaha to Denver to avoid being drafted into the Union Army during the Civil War. Hardin acknowledged her charges as true. But he declared their marriage illegal and void because he was a minor at that time and she was a slave.

Although Hardin was never officially charged with such crimes, the scandal led mint officials to fire him. With Nellie, Hardin moved that same fall of 1873 to Cheyenne, where he spent the next ten years in the tonsorial trade. In Cheyenne Hardin's pleasing personality and gift of gab won many new friends of diverse ethnic backgrounds. So many, in fact, that they elected him as their representative in 1879 to the Wyoming's Sixth Legislative Assembly, no small feat in a state where only three percent of the population declared their ethnicity to 1880 census-takers as "Negro." Praising his victory, a *Cheyenne Daily Sun* reporter cheered in a November 9, 1879, article that Hardin "has broken down race prejudice...by pre-eminent manifestations of ability and upright conduct."

Despite his fine service on behalf of the people, Hardin barely won a second term in the Wyoming House of Representatives. In the November 2, 1880, election he finished eighth among eighteen candidates, receiving 1,277 votes, a mere fifty-eight more than his closest rival. Nonetheless, he survived as the only House member of the Sixth Legislative Assembly to serve during the Seventh. His tenure ended December 31, 1883.

The following year, for reasons not clear, the Hardins packed their bags and moved to Park City, Utah, where their once-fiery celebrity faded, first to ember, then to ash. Nellie left William and, as his business and health failed, the once-great orator lost the last of his luck one day at the cabin he shared with a male friend. Sadly, he only found peace with a self-inflicted .38-caliber bullet to his heart on Friday, September 13, 1889.

⚭ SOURCES CITED ⚭ I gained insight regarding some of William Jefferson Hardin's early years from my December 31, 1997, interview with Dwight Middlebrook of Lowell, Massachusetts, whose great-great-aunt was Hardin's first wife, Caroline Catherine Butcher.

Most of the information for this story, however, came from the following articles: Eugene H. Berwanger's "William J. Hardin: Colorado Spokesman for Social Justice," *Colorado Magazine* (Vol. 52, No. 1), Winter 1975; Roger D. Hardaway's "William Jefferson Hardin: Wyoming's 19th Century Black Legislator," *Annals of Wyoming* (Vol. 63, No. 1), Winter 1991; and Hardin's untitled biographical article in the *Cheyenne Daily Sun*, November 1879.

Perhaps the saddest, most poignant views of Hardin's life, however, are contained in those newspaper articles that detailed his death: "Tired of Living," *The Park Record*, Park City, Utah, September 14, 1889, and "Suicide," *Cheyenne Daily Sun*, September 15, 1889.

This chapter first appeared, in a slightly different form, in the *Casper Star-Tribune*, February 8, 1999.

CHAPTER 45

Justice of the Peace
Esther Hobart Morris

CALICO JUSTICE IN SOUTH PASS CITY

THOSE WHO CAME before her court often found the calico-clad judge wearing a green tie, with her hair beribboned in the same hue. Her spouse and sons knew the big-boned, six-foot-tall woman as wife and mother. But the world perhaps best recalls Esther Hobart Morris as the "Mother of Women's Suffrage."

What many do not know is that she also served as the first-ever woman justice of the peace and presided as such in her log home at South Pass City, Wyoming. How that came to pass sometimes surprises even her most ardent admirers.

Shortly after the First Legislative Assembly gave Wyoming women the right to vote in December 1869, James W. Stillman, the South Pass City justice of the peace, sent a note in a fit of pique to the Sweetwater County Board of Commissioners:

> Sirs:
>
> In deference to the wisdom of our honourable legislators for our virgin territory and very respectable minority of the people of the United States in favor of female suffrage, and not wishing to be found backward in so laudable a cause, I therefore make this my resignation of the office of justice of the peace for Sweetwater county, Wyoming, to take effect whenever some lady elector shall have been duly appointed to fill the vacancy.

The next day, the commissioners accepted the sarcastic Stillman's challenge and voted two to one to accept his resignation. Wyoming's Secretary of State Edward M. Lee, with Governor John A. Campbell's blessing, quickly offered Esther Morris the vacant justice position.

231

Esther Hobart Morris, known as the "Mother of Women's Suffrage," was also the world's first female justice of the peace. (Wyoming State Archives)

Ironically, the first defendant she ordered to appear before her rough, wood-slab bench was her petulant predecessor. The charge? "Refusing to turn over records." Stillman balked at surrendering his official docket, saying, "No woman should have it." Esther Morris questioned, too, some alleged financial deficiencies, including the whereabouts of fines collected by Stillman. When he failed to provide satisfactory answers, Mrs. Morris issued a warrant on February 14, 1870, that brought him before the bar. He waited two days to respond, then moved that she dismiss the charge due to the "informality of warrant." When she turned that trick aside, the clever Stillman countered by demanding that she quash the case "on the ground of no jurisdiction and informality of information"—that is, lack of formal written accusation. While the inexperienced justice might have prevailed, common sense told her that as a key player in the feud, it would be a conflict of interest if she tried the case. So she told him to keep the record and wisely went on with her life. Later she said she really didn't want the "dirty docket," and her first son Edward, who became her clerk, bought her a "nice clean one."

Esther Morris also explained to friends that she "felt embarrassed" when authorities appointed her to an office she had not sought and to duties of which she "was practically ignorant." In fact, she did not want the position, she said, and would have preferred to see her husband get the job. But when Mr. Morris later found fault with her handling of that first case, the not-so-shy woman replied, "My dear, if you had been sitting in the chair, you could have rendered your own decision."

Despite her claim that she never felt comfortable sitting in judgment, she rose to the challenge and heard at least nine criminal cases—including one for assault, six for assault and battery, and two for assault with intent to kill— during her one-year term.

To what can we attribute Esther Morris's strength of character and confidence that served her so well? It helps to look at her early years.

She was born August 8, 1812, near Spencer in Tioga County, New York, as the eighth of Daniel and Charlotte Hobart McQuigg's eleven children. Orphaned at fourteen, she worked as a milliner in neighboring Oswego before, at age twenty-eight, she wed civil engineer Artemus Slack in 1841. There the couple had a son, Edward Archibald (E.A.), on October 2 of the following year.

Artemus died in 1846, however, leaving his widow and infant son an inheritance that included a tract of land in Peru, Illinois. After moving there to manage her affairs, she met John Morris, a Polish immigrant and prominent local merchant. They married and Esther gave birth to three more sons: John, Jr., who died in infancy, and twins Robert C. and Edward J. on November 8, 1851.

John Morris and young E.A. Slack—now in his mid-twenties—moved in 1868 to South Pass City, a rowdy mining town, where Morris searched for gold and also opened a saloon. His fifty-six-year-old wife followed that July with their twins and almost immediately took an active part in community affairs. In fact, shortly before the September 2 election that year, she hosted a party for some forty guests at their home. After tea Mrs. Morris suggested to Republican Herman G. Nickerson and Democrat William H. Bright, both candidates for the legislature, that whoever won office should introduce a suffrage bill. Both promised, but as the winner, Bright proposed the act which on December 10, 1869, became the first such law anywhere guaranteeing women the right to vote. Esther Morris's reward for that suggestion was the justice of the peace appointment.

But soon after she left the bench in 1870, domestic difficulties caused her to split from her husband and she soon joined her son E.A., who had moved to Laramie. There, the following year, he founded and published the *Laramie Daily Independent.* While residing with her sons in the "Gem City," Esther Morris attended a few national suffrage conventions, including one in 1872 at San Francisco, where she made a few remarks but "no attempt at a speech." The women of Laramie even nominated her to run for the legislature in 1873, but she chose not to accept that honor. Three years passed and she followed E.A. to Cheyenne, where he established himself as publisher of the *Cheyenne Sun* and, in 1880, joined it with the *Cheyenne Leader* to form the *Cheyenne Sun-Leader.* Esther lived periodically with him and his family. She spent time, too, with Robert, a bachelor who now also worked in the capital city as a clerk-reporter for the Wyoming Supreme Court.

The first public suggestion that Esther Hobart Morris's fame reached beyond being the first female justice of the peace came at the 1889 Constitutional Convention in Cheyenne. Its president, Melville C. Brown erred, while discussing voting rights, by claiming that she first presented the suffrage bill to the legislature. Apparently, based on Brown's remarks, her proud son E.A. began to boast and boost his mother in his newspaper as the "Mother of Suffrage." The well-known suffragist Dr. Grace Hebard (see chapter 19: A Source and Subject of Wyoming History"), a University of Wyoming faculty member, also waved that banner both to immortalize Esther Morris as a hero and to promote national suffrage, a cause in which both women played prominent roles.

Despite her advancing years, Esther Morris still found energy and mobility, with the aid of a cane, to participate in those causes most dear to her, even representing Wyoming at the 1894 National Republican Convention in Cleveland, Ohio. Six years later, her life ended peacefully on April 2, 1902—four months short of her ninetieth birthday—in Cheyenne, where family buried her in the Lakeview Cemetery. Thanks to bronze statues in her likeness, later placed to honor her at Statuary Hall in Washington, D.C., and in front of Wyoming's State Capitol, her image lives on—as does the memory of her deeds on behalf of women.

❧ SOURCES CITED ❧ Following my January 28, 1998, interview with Esther Hobart Morris's great-grandson William Dubois in Cheyenne, from whom I gained valuable family information, I referred to a wide variety of secondary sources for more details on her life and times. These publications and articles include Paul Friggen's "The Lady Who Wanted to Vote," *Denver Post*, October 24, 1943; *Wyoming State Parks & Historic Sites* brochure (Cheyenne: Wyoming Department of Commerce, 1997); and T.A. Larson's *History of Wyoming* (Lincoln, NE: University of Nebraska Press, 1978). The Wyoming State Archives holdings include "Esther Hobart Morris," Microfilm [MA #6539], August 19, 1975, Sweetwater County, Vol. I; the collection "Esther Morris, Justice of the Peace, South Pass City, Wyoming," February 14, 1870-October 20, 1871. A biographical file titled "Esther Hobart Morris," [B-M321-e] can be found in the Grace Raymond Hebard Collection at the University of Wyoming in Laramie. Another indispensable work is Michael A. Massie's "Reform Is Where You Find It: The Roots of Woman Suffrage in Wyoming," *Annals of Wyoming* (Vol. 62, No. 1), Spring 1990.

This chapter first appeared, in a slightly different form, in the *Casper Star-Tribune*, March 8, 1998.

CHAPTER 46

BRIGHAM YOUNG AND HIS FOLLOWERS

A TALE OF THOSE ON THE MORMON TRAIL

A BUGLE BLARED THROUGH the chilly darkness, calling William Clayton from the warmth of his blankets. After worshiping at his wagon, he made and ate breakfast before feeding his ox team for that day's pull across the prairie.

Throughout the camp just inside Wyoming's eastern border, 142 kindred souls—including three women and two children—accompanied by fifty-two mules, sixty-six oxen, nineteen cows, seventeen dogs, and a flock of chickens, joined him in preparing for their continued westward search for a home. As Clayton wrote in his journal, they sought a place where "the saints can live in peace…not under the dominion of gentile governments, and… enjoy the fullness of the gospel."

The date? June 1, 1847. Before sunset, the caravan of twenty-five wagons would be halfway "there."

Traveling terrain that tested their faith as well as their mettle, the trail Clayton and his fellow Mormons followed was seldom smooth. Ever since the vision of Joseph Smith, their leader, had called him to restore "the true Christianity," persecutors had driven Smith and his followers west, from New York to Ohio and Missouri, and finally to Illinois. There, in the city of Carthage, a mob, suspicious of the sect's economic and political power and its practice of polygamy, murdered Smith on June 10, 1844.

With the proverbial "hounds of hell" at their heels, the brethren fled under the direction of Brigham Young—Smith's successor—to the west bank of the Missouri River, north of Omaha, Nebraska, where they spent the winter of 1846.

Many pioneers who passed through Wyoming, including Brigham Young and his Latter-Day Saints, scratched names and dates on the famed Independence Rock. This sketch by William Henry Jackson also shows the V-shaped Devil's Gate (left center) through which passed the Oregon Trail. (Wyoming State Archives)

The following spring, even before the geese flew north, Young and his followers crossed the "Mighty Mo" on April 7 and went west in search of their Zion.

By traveling the north bank of the Platte River, rather than risk conflicts on the south side with travelers who did not share their faith, Clayton and others in the Pioneer Party found themselves roughly 510 miles west of their winter home on the first of June. At the second bugle call that morning, with the weather warm and fair, the group crossed Rawhide Creek and continued upstream while hugging the high, sandy buff-colored hills along the river.

Finally, at about eleven-thirty, the Mormons halted for lunch, having traveled only about four and a half miles. Clayton recorded their difficult progress in his diary:

> *The road today has been sandy and heavy on teams with but little feed in any place. The country begins to have a more*

hilly and mountainous appearance. Some of the Black Hills [now called Wyoming's Laramie Range; not South Dakota's Black Hills] show very plain from here. The timber is mostly ash and cottonwood on the low bottoms near the river. There is some cedar on the bluffs.

Shortly after four that afternoon, while riding point on a borrowed horse, Clayton saw Fort Laramie about four miles to the southwest; the site was then a trading post and not yet a military fort. After sending back word of his find, Clayton recorded:

President Young then came up to where Brother Woodruff and I were looking out for feed and we started on, President Young having stopped the wagons, and went to the ford opposite the fort. It was finally concluded to form our encampment here on the banks of the river.

At the end of most days, the Mormons pulled their wagons into a circle, forming a corral to protect themselves and their stock. But this afternoon, thanks to their proximity to the fort, they pulled their rigs into the shape of a V abutting the river. Soon thereafter, seeing some men ride out from the fort, Young and several of his party crossed the river in a portable "sole leather" boat to meet them and exchange news. Their guests, according to Clayton, "made themselves known as part of the Mississippi company [of Mormons] from Pueblo [Colorado]…It caused us much joy to meet with brethren in this wild region of the country."

At about nine the next morning, President Young and other leaders of his group again launched their small boat, crossed the broad Platte, and walked two miles upstream to Fort Laramie. Clayton recounted his first impressions of the place, referring to James Bordeaux with a variant spelling:

It stands on the bank of the Laramie fork…A stream forty-one yards wide, a very swift current, but not deep…We are politely welcomed by Mr. Bordeau who appears to be the principal officer. He conducted us up a flight of stairs into a comfortable *room and being furnished with seats, we rested ourselves. President Young and others entered into conversation with Mr. Bordeau. From him learned that we cannot travel over four miles farther on the north side of the Platte before we come to bluffs which cannot be crossed with loaded wagons. The road is better on this [south] side than the one we have traveled, it being hard and not sandy. Feed scarce mostly lying in little patches near the river… They have got a flat boat which will carry two wagons easily [in] which… he [Bordeaux] will ferry us over for $18.00 …From the door of this room we can see the same black hill seen on Sunday evening and which is Laramie Peak. We could see the snow lying on it very plainly. We can also see several ranges of high hills in the distance which are no doubt parts of the Black Hills.*

Continuing in his diary, Clayton wrote:

We went across the square to the trading house which lies on the north side of the western entrance. The trader opened his store and President Young entered into conversation with him … The blacksmith shop lies on the south side of the western entrance. There are dwellings inside the fort beside that of Mr. Bordeau's. The south end is divided off and occupied for stables, etc.

Clayton concluded, "There are many souls at this fort, mostly French, half-breeds, and a few Sioux Indians."

While their leaders were visiting the fort, the rest of the Mormons, starting at dawn, inspected their equipment and repaired damaged parts. Their makeshift forges were fired by charcoal which they made by burning in pits birch and willow wood collected from the nearby riverbanks. The Pioneer Party spent most of the next day shuttling their wagons across the river, at first averaging one every fifteen minutes. Then a strong southeast wind swept heavy rains and hail through the area. By the time the squall subsided that evening, fifteen wagons still remained on the north side of the river.

Water caught in a small crevice on the top northeast corner of Independence Rock—the "Great Register of the Desert"—leads the eye to the inscription "Milo J. Ayer, age 29, 1849." (Wyoming State Archives)

But by about eight the next morning—June 4—the brethren ferried the last wagon to the other side of the swollen Platte. Then, after paying one last call on Bordeaux at the fort, where they received a final briefing regarding upcoming trail and weather conditions, Young and his followers made ready for the last half of their journey. At noon, with Laramie Peak looming darkly on the horizon, the pioneers—joined by the seventeen brethren from Pueblo—resumed their journey.

Forty-eight days later—Thursday, July 22—after having traveled roughly a thousand miles from their winter quarters on the Missouri River, Clayton broached the top of a hill where he "was much cheered," he wrote, "by a handsome view of the Great Salt Lake lying...25 to 30 miles to the west." Thus ended the first wave of the Latter-Day Saints' exodus to a "Promised Land," where they still thrive and prosper.

✤ SOURCES CITED ✤ Among the many sources used to prepare this story, certainly the most valuable was W. [William] Clayton's *The Latter-Day Saints' Emigrants' Guide: Being a Table of Distances, Showing All the Springs, Creeks, Rivers, Hills, Mountains, Camping Places, and All Other Notable Places, from Council Bluffs, to the Valley of the Great Salt Lake* (St. Louis, MO: Republic Steam Power Press-Chambers & Knapp, 1848).

Nearly as important was *William Clayton's Journal, A Daily Record of the Journey of the Original Company of "Mormon" Pioneers from Nauvoo, Illinois, to the Valley of the Great Salt Lake* (Salt Lake City: The Deseret News, reprinted from the original in 1921).

Other significant sources include Maurine Carley's "Oregon Trail Trek No. One," *Annals of Wyoming* (Vol. 27, No. 2), October 1955; Dale L. Morgan's "The Mormon Ferry on the North Platte; The Journal of William A. Empey, May 7- August 4, 1847," *Annals of Wyoming* (Vol. 21, Nos. 2-3), July-October 1949; and *Fort Laramie National Monument*, (Washington, D.C.: U.S. Department of the Interior, 1942).

This chapter first appeared, in a slightly different form, in the *Casper Star-Tribune*, February 1, 1998.

CHAPTER 47

Wyoming's First Families

MEMORIES OF THE HISTORIC GOVERNOR'S MANSION

Some see the big red-brick house only as a relic of the past. For a few it is a shrine to those who for seventy years lived in the elegant Georgian-style estate. But the twenty surviving offspring of Wyoming's chief executives simply recall the two-and-a-half-story Historic Governor's Mansion as "home."

Take Silas Brooks, one of the first children to live at the corner of East Twenty-first Street and House Avenue in Cheyenne. The only son of Governor Bryant B. (whose term spanned 1905–11) and Mary Naomi Brooks loved to fish in the early morn with his next-door neighbor, David Cook. But the governor soon tired of being jolted from sleep when young Dave rang the doorbell. To end that annoyance, the boys devised a plan. Si tied a long cord to one of his big toes and dropped it from his second-floor bedroom window to the front steps. From then on, Dave just pulled the string to rouse his pal from bed.

The first of nineteen families to live in the mansion, which the state built for $3,700 in 1904, the Brooks clan was also the youngest and the largest. With five tots under its roof, the abode also served as their playground. Si and his four sisters performed plays in the top-floor rooms and held track meets in the spacious basement.

Later children of Wyoming's first families also took pleasure in the place. David Emerson, son of Governor Frank C. and Zennia Emerson (1927–31), loved to shoot baskets with friends at the backyard hoop. Francis "Frank" and James—sons of Governor Frank A. and Alice Barrett (1951–53)—clearly recall the day of their dad's inauguration. They listened to the radio broadcast that afternoon as the University of Wyoming's football team trounced Washington & Lee 20–7 at the Gator Bowl in Florida: the Cowboys' first-ever bowl game.

Even a few pets found comfort on the state's great estate. The Brooks daughters loved to tell of their pet pony which they kept in the carriage house they could see from their second-floor bedroom window. Governor Frank and Ida Houx's (1917–19) four tots held "circuses" in the basement where their menagerie performed tricks for family and neighbors. Perhaps none of those four-footed friends proved as messy as "Mickey," David Emerson's Irish setter, who gave birth to a litter of pups on the seat of one of the mansion's fine chairs.

Nights at the mansion might be memorable times, too. Governor Stanley K. and Roberta "Bobby" Hathaway's (1967–75) girls—Susan and Sandra—endured a thunderstorm one night that dropped a ceiling beam, revealing a rusty sword hidden in the wall. And the sons of Governor Milward L. and Lorna Simpson (1955–59) —Pete and Alan—suffered beds too small for their respective six-foot, four-inch and six-foot, seven-inch frames.

Many of the youngsters fondly remember the mansion's staff. Frank Barrett recalls finding his old schoolteacher and former University of Wyoming football star Jesse Ekdall there in 1951. Six years earlier, authorities had sent Ekdall—by then Cheyenne's Chief of Police—to work as the mansion's maintenance man after they convicted him of corruption and bribery. But perhaps the best-remembered staff are housekeepers Johneana "Janeen" Scribner, who worked there sixteen years, and "sweet, affable" Mary Stephen, who served six administrations at the mansion and two more at the current governor's residence near Kiwanis Lake.

Lavish celebrations and a near-steady stream of visiting celebrities added to the place's lustrous history. High on the list of "most memorable" events was the champagne wedding reception hosted by Governor Lester C. and Nathelle Hunt (1943–49) for their daughter Elise and her groom, First Lieutenant H.W. Chadwick. Elise and her brother "Buddy" still speak with excitement about President Harry

The Historic Governor's Mansion, at the corner of East Twenty-first Street and House Avenue in Cheyenne, served from 1905 to 1976 as home of nineteen of Wyoming's twenty-two "First Families" (Wyoming State Archives)

Truman's visit in June 1948. And nearly all of the children who lived in the mansion remember best the parties their parents threw for state legislators. David Emerson, as well as the brothers Barrett, Hickey, and Simpson, still laugh about how they helped as "coat boys" and served refreshments. Young Peter Simpson sometimes entertained guests by singing and playing folk and western music on his guitar.

Over the decades, many first families physically improved the property. Governor John B. Kendrick replaced the original drawing-room fireplace mantel in 1914 with the oak-paneled mantel and over-chimney piece that remain today. "Kendrick also replaced all of the original brass combination lighting fixtures with all-electric fixtures," said curator Timothy White. "These combination fixtures were two-armed: one arm used electricity, the other gas. When frequent brownouts and electrical failures occurred, the gas arm could then be lit as a backup system." When Leslie A. Miller became governor

Governor Bryant B. Brooks, his wife Mary, and their children pose on the porch of their home at their V-V ranch before moving as First Family into the new Governor's Mansion in 1905. (Wyoming State Archive)

in 1933, White said, "he eliminated two bedrooms and one of the original two bathrooms on the second floor, and replaced them with three new bathrooms and five large closets. Since 1937, the second floor has had four bedrooms, each with a full bath."

Other governors enhanced the home's symbolic features. Governor Hunt established a photo collection featuring Wyoming's First Ladies. Governor Simpson wanted one room to reflect Wyoming's land and people, so he commissioned Thomas Molesworth of Cody to build a set of furniture for his den (see chapter 8: "Molesworth Furniture, the Best in the West"). Made of native pine and cedar, the upholstered pieces feature embroidered pine boughs and Indian paintbrush, Wyoming's state flower. The den, since renamed "The Wyoming Room," remains unchanged. Later the Hathaways, too, left their mark by establishing the first Governor's Mansion Library featuring Wyoming authors.

Some rooms evolved over time. The Simpsons created an open-air sun porch off the second floor. Simpson's successor, J.J. "Joe" Hickey (1959–61) and his spouse, Winifred, enclosed the porch to make it a year-round family room. Then, when Clifford P. Hansen was sworn in as governor in 1963, he and his wife, Martha, installed the silk curtains and hand-screened damask-patterned wallpaper which remain today.

Another noticeable addition is the stair-elevator installed by Governor Ed Herschler during his term (1975–87). It helped his wife, Casey, who had multiple sclerosis (MS), move to and from the first floor to their private quarters on the second floor. Their daughter Sue, recalled that her children loved to ride the lift each time they visited their grandparents at the mansion.

Restoration, according to curator White, has been a major focus since the mansion became a state museum site in July 1977. Three bedrooms have been restored. Some of the original 1905 furnishings, now repurchased, are on display. In 1986–87, the entrance hall was restored to its 1905 decor, including the re-installation of a pair of brass, combination-style ceiling fixtures. A permanent exhibit of photographs donated by Wyoming's First Families has been established, and these pictures illustrate, in a graphic and personal way, the many chapters of the building's history.

❧ SOURCES CITED ❧ No visit to Cheyenne is complete without a stop at the Historic Governor's Mansion.

And no writer should focus on that most elegant abode without talking to some of those who lived there. So, in addition to repeated visits and interviews with the curator, Timothy White, I also talked or corresponded during 1998 with many one-time inhabitants; notes from those interviews are in the author's files.

A good understanding of the mansion's history is also offered by Timothy White's superb "Wyoming's Historic Governor's Mansion," *Annals of Wyoming* (Vol. 61, No. 1), Spring 1989.

This chapter first appeared, in a slightly different form, in the *Casper Star-Tribune*, April 12, 1998.

CHAPTER 48

Mary Ada Fisher, aka Dell Burke

LUSTY LADY OF LUSK

T HE RICH SCENT of fast food and the happy chatter of the crowd calling bids to the auctioneers gave the estate sale a carnival air. But for the friends of Dell Burke, it failed to entertain. Rather, the sordid little wake made them sad.

Most of those who shopped beneath the bright broad sky that weekend in August 1981 in Lusk, Wyoming, had once felt so shy of Dell that they crossed the street to avoid her shadow. Now they sought traces of her, peeking behind her red velvet drapes where little more than the brass room keys, naughty nighties, and pastel silk hose remained. The Dell who had ruled there had died. She had been gone, in fact, for nearly a year.

The petite, auburn-haired beauty entered life as Mary Ada Fisher on July 5, 1888, in Somerset, Ohio, about thirty miles southeast of Columbus. Soon thereafter, a pastor of the Somerset Lutheran Parish baptized her, the only daughter of John and Almeda (Cotterman) Fisher and the youngest of their four children.

In the winter of 1897, Mary's family learned that her uncle Charles, who had settled in Dakota Territory, had died in a blizzard. While settling his estate, her parents, too, became infected by the homesteading fever. The following spring, John Fisher and his family boarded a westbound train—their household goods in one car and their livestock in another—and headed for North Dakota. Stopping first on the Tongue River at Cavalier, they lived briefly in a boxcar provided by the railroad. Dell remembered with pride that her mother kept that home-on-wheels as "neat as a pin."

247

Six-year-old Mary Fisher poses precociously at her father John's knee. This family portrait with her mother Almeda and brothers (from left) Herbert, Charles, and Burl, was taken in a Somerset, Ohio, studio around 1894. (Loraine A. Fisher collection)

The family soon continued west, however, arriving at Rolla on April 7, 1898. The hotels there were full so Rolette County officials boarded them and other passengers in the local courthouse, equipping them with stoves for cooking and heating. Several days later the Fishers moved on to Wolf Creek, a small township twenty-three miles south of the Canadian border. There, John bought two 160-acre parcels, one in his own name and one in his wife's. The cost? A grand total of $51.20, or sixteen cents an acre. A trusting man in the area lent that money to John. Having been a merchant in Ohio, John built the Fisher Store and Post Office later that year at what would be known, during its brief existence, as Fisher, North Dakota.

The apple of her daddy's eye, Mary enrolled at age thirteen at St. Bernard's Academy in Grand Forks. There she received an elementary

Fisher, North Dakota, consisted of a combination store and post office which John Fisher built soon after moving into the Wolf Creek area in April 1898. (Loraine A. Fisher collection)

education from Mother Superior Stanislaus Rafter and her Ursuline nuns. The opportunity to leave home and stretch her wings must have seemed exciting at first to Mary, as she and her girlfriends spent much of their free time standing on the convent fence calling to boys at the nearby college. But with the passage of puberty Marie—as she preferred to be called—apparently found the strict religious environment too confining and welcomed the chance to rejoin her family.

The Fishers in the meantime had sold their property in 1905 to the "Soo" (Minneapolis, St. Paul and Sault Ste. Marie) Railway. After a brief visit back East to see their relatives, they returned to North Dakota, this time to Bottineau County. They settled in Omemee, about twenty miles west of their previous home in Fisher. Seventeen-year-old Marie took a job handling weigh bills and other paperwork at the local depot where she met Stephen J. Law, seven years her senior. The Canadian railroad freight conductor and his young love, who swore her age was a legal eighteen, wed November 12, 1905, in Grafton, in the northeast corner of the state. Moving into her new home there, Marie met the sister with whom her husband had long shared the house. That strong-willed sibling soon

Marie and Stephen J. Law, a Canadian railroad freight conductor, were married on November 12, 1905, in Grafton, North Dakota. The seventeen-year-old bride stretched the truth when she swore she was eighteen, the legal age to wed. (Loraine A. Fisher collection)

overwhelmed the new bride. Fed up, too, with her jealous spouse's boasts that "Canadians are better than Americans," Marie left the following year to seek a life on her own.

Traveling northwest to Calgary, Alberta, Marie went to work at the famed resort hotel at Banff. There she endeared herself to the local police chief and his son, who protected her from Stephen's pursuit. But the amorous advances of the lawman's son proved more difficult to avoid than those of her husband. With a limited income and faced with a new entanglement as untenable as the one she had left behind, Marie made a decision that would lead her into an unfamiliar nether world.

Mary Ada Fisher Law, aka Dell Burke, ruled as Lusk's "Lusty Lady" for sixty-three years. (Loraine A. Fisher collection)

Although it is not clear why Marie chose the course she did, probably she needed money. The attractive woman also found men unusually vulnerable to her charms. Taking a wider perspective, one may understand how the social economics of her era contributed to her fall from grace. An ambitious female of that time, regardless of her station, had few options for personal or professional self-expression and independence. An affluent lady, of course, could bask in the accomplishments of her husband or son. And a lucky few gained celebrity as hostesses, sponsors of artists and musicians, or promoters of charitable causes. But for a single woman, especially one still under twenty and without independent means, survival proved a challenge. A fortunate one might be skilled in sewing or crafts. With special training, some could aspire to teach or nurse. Lacking those choices, others might face more extreme options: entering either a religious order or the "world's oldest profession," prostitution. Marie chose the latter. It required little or no investment. A low-watt lamp

Dell Burke, already infamous for the life she led, posed for this portrait in 1914 at a professional photographer's Seattle studio soon after the Juneau boom went bust and she left Alaska. (Loraine A. Fisher collection)

and a wrought-iron bed could be magically transformed with a look and a smile into cold, hard cash. Marie assumed the first of several stage names and followed the call of the wild to Alaska.

She made that journey at a most propitious time. Her livelihood was coming under attack in the States by what became known as the Progressive Movement. The seeds of mid-nineteenth century English socialism had taken root in America, first in its northeastern seaboard cities. But the wave of reform that followed would sweep across the land. The Progressives first introduced a system of community guilds and settlements that they hoped would correct the class distinctions and social ills they believed came with urbanism and industrialization. These included such programs as the National Child Labor Committee, the National Women's Trade Union

League, the National Association for the Advancement of Colored People, the Playground Association, the National Conference on City Planning, and the National Conference on Charities and Corrections. They also lobbied for a federal investigation on women and children in the industrial workforce. Their ideas and initiatives proved so forceful that, from their numbers and influence, a political party—the Progressive Party—formed.

The Progressives hoped to stamp out such vices as gambling, alcohol abuse, and prostitution that exacerbated other, greater problems. They aimed to turn schools, parks, and libraries into social centers that would supplant saloons and brothels. Thus, what Victorians had discreetly regarded as the necessary evils of human nature, turn-of-the-century Americans came to view as social evils, moral problems, and national menaces.

They also believed that low wages led to lax moral conditions among young women. Public anxiety over promiscuity and other unacceptable behavior peaked during 1911–16 as prostitution became linked to every imaginable form of individual and public corruption. Also linking alcoholic beverages to other "houses of ill repute" such as dance halls and saloons, Progressives crusaded against such evils to prevent further exploitation of women and children. They simultaneously established more playgrounds and social centers. Just as Dell thought those moralists might take away her livelihood, she turned her eyes north and tackled the next chapter in her young life.

In Juneau, the hub of Yukon gold-boom traffic, Marie learned a lesson that served her well: nature hates a vacuum, particularly an absence of women. Alaska had, during the early 1900s, a ratio of one woman to every one hundred men. Given her unhappy marital experience, Marie must have felt extraordinarily special in a land where, according to physician Earl F. Nation, "A white woman is treated everywhere on the Pacific slope, not as a man's equal and companion, but as a strange and costly creature, which by virtue of its rarity is freed from the restraints and penalties of ordinary law."

She remembered Saturday nights as especially grand, as Alaska's governor and state legislators drank and socialized in the

254 ᱻ Coyotes & Canaries

establishment where she worked. Some, she said later, engaged in more than verbal intercourse.

So, in that far-away land of the midnight sun, Marie struck pay dirt—big-time. Within one year she had made ten thousand dollars. An aggressive, unwanted suitor also gave her a gold and diamond ring, but Marie declared her independence by throwing his gift into the icy Yukon River.

Soon thereafter, as the boom went bust and the hostile cold took its toll, Marie and Bess Housley, a girlfriend, moved south in 1914 to Seattle. Not long after, however, puritanical Progressive pressures as well as the girls' own "quest for the best" drove them toward Portland, Oregon. They soon continued to Butte, Montana, where they learned of America's entry into World War I and found work in their trade. While at Butte, Dell later claimed, a wealthy stockgrower from Dixon, North Dakota, nearly kidnapped her. Without telling Marie, he paid her madam a handsome price, planning to take the young prostitute away to his ranch. Marie probably believed, when he took her from the house where she worked, that they were going out on a date. Instead, he led her to the train depot where he explained the deal he had made. But Marie refused to go. When he tried to pull her aboard the train, she broke from his grasp and ran to nearby police for protection.

Learning of the famed Salt Creek Field boom, Marie and her girlfriend followed the trail of oil and money in late 1917 or early 1918 to Casper, Wyoming. There they set up shop in time to celebrate the World War I armistice in the notorious, vice-ridden Sandbar district. When they first arrived at that new addition to the west edge of the city, its wild and wooly lifestyle must have rivaled that of Alaska in its gold-rush heyday. But the Progressive wave of moral reform sweeping America finally reached the high plains in the form of Prohibition. In 1918, Wyoming adopted the Eighteenth Amendment by a vote of more than three to one. The state would go bone-dry on July 1, 1919.

Anticipating the law's passage, Casper city fathers had met in closed session in February 1919 and declared that the Sandbar

Dell Burke, following her success as a prostitute during the gold rush days in the Yukon, worked in brothels in Washington, Oregon, and Montana before settling in Wyoming in 1917. (Loraine A. Fisher Collection)

... is and has been for some time a rendezvous for all manner of crooks and criminals, a breeding ground for vice of every character, where state statutes are violated with impunity, intoxicating liquors being sold without license in illegal resorts, practically every form of vice flourishing without restraint.

The next month, those councilmen declared a war on vice by passing an ordinance making it illegal for prostitutes to be on the streets, in doorways or windows, or anywhere else subject to public view between 7 A.M. and 7 P.M. By the end of March, 224 arrests had been made, the most for any single month at that point in Casper's history. Spurred that summer by local mavens of morality, the council determined that nine Sandbar resorts selling liquor without a license should be shut down. In Natrona County's first bootlegging raid, police found stills from which they confiscated thousands of gallons of wine, beer, and whisky.

Although Wyoming's weather much improved Marie's spirits, she felt too much heat from the increased law enforcement. Marie knew from experience that it was time, again, to hit the road. So she and Bessie went east to Lusk, Wyoming, where a populace of ten thousand bobbed happily on the crest of the Lance Creek oil wave.

Arriving in early 1919 at the age of thirty, with her health and good looks, she found herself in the midst of more men than she could easily count. "Lusk is what Casper was!" she may have thought. In fact, with a hearty laugh, she told a reporter in later years, "I thought the name of the place was 'Lust.' That's one of the reasons I came." Sporting her latest alias, Dell Burke, she and her girlfriend set up shop in a tent where they serviced their customers. One morning soon after, Lusk mayor J. E. Mayes agreed to rent her a house where she and her soiled doves went to work that same afternoon. About a year later, on January 5, 1920, Dell and Bessie Housley bought a two-story stucco building at 219 West First Street (now Griffith Boulevard), next to the railroad tracks on the north side of town.

The flesh peddler's entrepreneurial flair for marketing was obvious. She introduced her new talent to the community by having each girl stroll down the street carrying Dell's beloved Pekingese in her arms. Dell "was a real good-hearted old girl," one Lusk man fondly said. "The girls weren't too shiny when she got hold of them. She cleaned them up and dressed them and made them look like real good looking ladies."

Their accommodations included ten bedrooms on the top floor of the freshly-painted, yellow bagnio known as the "Yellow Hotel." According to a patron, a central north-south hall separated rooms on either side. Dell's modest apartment consisted of a parlor, living room, bath, and bedroom linked like train cars along the east side of the ground floor. Because the hotel stood near the depot, sometimes little old ladies came to town, saw her sign, and knocked on the front door in search of a room. Dell, always polite, simply told them she had no vacancies and sent them on down the street. Kids on their way to the local swimming hole also found the hotel along

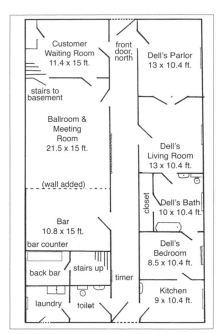

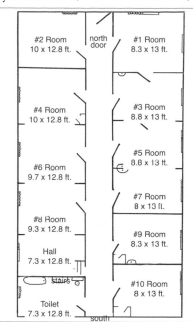

The Yellow Hotel's floor plan, as sketched by the author, shows Dell Burke's railroad-style living quarters along the east side of the building. Her girls did their business in ten bedrooms on the second floor.

their path. One old-timer recalled, "When I was a kid…it was just an automatic detour to see what was going on at Dell's. It was fascinating because it was a no-no. Dell would see us and say, 'You boys ought not be here!' and she'd chase us off."

Despite passage of the Volstead Act in October 1919 that provided for the enforcement of the Eighteenth Amendment prohibiting the sale, manufacture, or transportation of intoxicating liquors, such beverages continued to be indispensable to the brothel business. "When this place was booming," Dell said, "money was plentiful, so were women, booze and gambling." To ensure an ample supply of moonshine containers, Dell hired boys to scavenge the area around local halls such as the "Merry Whirl" after Saturday-night dances. She paid five cents for each empty half-pint liquor bottle. When one youngster managed to sneak some hootch from Dell's own stash, she soon discovered the theft. Dell called the suspect at school and asked him to stop by her hotel after class. When

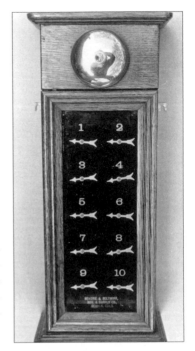

This timer hung on the wall at the foot of the stairs in the Yellow Hotel. The numbers identify the rooms in which Dell's clients were entertained. An arrow was set for each such customer and the bell signaled an end to his session. (Wyoming State Archives)

he arrived, Dell served the unsuspecting lad a soft drink before spending the next half hour praising his potential and lauding his parents. As he started to leave, she called him back and said, "Never steal from your friends." Although she said nothing more about the incident, the young man never forgot those parting words and the lesson they taught him.

While Dell understood the Golden Rule, she failed to heed laws regarding the illegal possession and sale of alcoholic beverages. She paid dearly when she ignored the following warning of John F. Kramer, the nation's first Prohibition Commissioner:

This law will be obeyed in cities, large and small, and in vil-lages, and where it is not obeyed it will be enforced. We shall see to it that it is not manufactured, nor sold, nor given away, nor hauled in anything over the surface of the earth or under the earth or in the air.

In support of such political posturing, one ardent Prohibition-ist advocate added, "The putting of the fear of God in the minds of

Dell and "Chi-Chi," her faithful Pekingese companion, share the running board of this vintage automobile. Each girl she hired introduced herself to the community by walking the street with Dell's pet in her arms. (Loraine A. Fisher Collection)

those who fear neither God nor man is the chief function of good government." During the Roaring Twenties, federal agents arrested some 577,000 suspects nationwide. Law-abiding Wyoming officials, like their federal counterparts, determined they would punish those who flagrantly violated federal liquor laws. From August 1928 to March 1929 they regularly busted Dell and those in her establishment. Their charges ran the gamut from illegal possession and sale of whisky to allegations of lewdness, prostitution, and gambling. The lawmen, however, clearly targeted alcohol-related crimes, and Dell wound up paying fines ranging from $25 to $300 per offense.

Determined to survive what she must have perceived as outrageous harassment, Dell concocted a scheme, probably with the help of her lawyer, that would offer relief. She learned that the Lusk light and power department in 1929 needed to quickly replace much of its equipment, including a 200-kilowatt engine and generator to supply the town's inhabitants with light and water. As the leaders of Lusk struggled to finance the replacement of $22,300 worth of vital machinery, Dell apparently came to the rescue with a personal loan to be repaid at six percent interest. Although Dell's name does not

260 Coyotes & Canaries

appear in public records, several officials confirmed that she "bailed us out when we were about to go under."

Mayor T.A. Godfrey and members of the city council seemed appreciative, too, but that did not prevent authorities beyond their influence and jurisdiction from enforcing Wyoming law. On March 11, 1930, Judge C.O. Brown of the Sixth Judicial District Court authorized an injunction that closed the Yellow Hotel for all but private dwelling purposes until the end of that year. Chastised, Dell decided to mend her ways and play the game...but with new rules. Although she left no paper trail, the popular opinion is that Dell lost no time in reminding city fathers that she held their loan. Unless they wanted her to shut off their water—literally as well as figuratively, since electricity powered the town's pump—they would be wise to let her reopen the Yellow Hotel without interference when the injunction ended the following December 31. Although Dell encountered no more official interference, those who saw her little black books detailing three generations of clients claimed that the Depression hurt her as much as anyone. "In 1933, there was a day when she only took in four dollars and the next day she only took in three dollars. But she always got cash—not checks," said Helen E. Brummell, a Torrington resident, who later helped prepare Dell's estate for sale.

Even the end of Prohibition that year offered only partial relief because, at first, only 3.2 percent beer could be lawfully sold in Wyoming. Not until April 1935 did state officials finally legalize stronger alcoholic drinks. But throughout the trying times, Dell could operate with relative impunity, perhaps because she knew many prominent people in the state. With an edge to her voice, Dell once said, "Oh, have I known people—have I known hypocrites." One civic leader confided that she had the town in the palm of her hand for years. "Maybe it's because I know too much for everybody's good," added Lusk's madam. "There are ten churches in town. But not a minister or a priest has ever preached against me so far as I know. And I've known them all on a first-name basis." Obviously Dell felt comfortable with the community's live-and-let-live attitude.

In a rare reunion with family members after she entered professional life, Dell (upper right) is pictured with her brothers Burl (left) and Charles. Her sister-in-law Nora (center), moved in 1931 to Lusk where she worked for Dell after her husband Charles mysteriously disappeared on a business trip. (Loraine A. Fisher collection)

As word of Dell's bordello spread, thanks in part to billboards posted on roads leading to Lusk, her stable of women stayed busy. Johns came from all points of the compass for flings on the well-worn mattresses of her wrought-iron beds. In the early years, the girls did business with oil-patch workers or well-heeled speculators for as little as two dollars a session, lasting from twenty minutes to an hour at Dell's discretion. Transient railroaders, hunters, and servicemen also visited the hotel where they danced with the girls to tunes played by a small orchestra. The madam always answered the front door herself and personally ejected drunk and disorderly clients. To avoid attention, men usually entered the back door before walking down the hall to the largest room in the house. There, they might first dance or just pick a partner before heading upstairs to the rooms. Dell used an electric timer with bells that signaled when it was time for the customers to leave. After satisfying their baser appetites, they usually dined, too, on what Dell bragged were Wyoming's best steak dinners, prepared by a Chinese cook.

Her clientele's greenbacks sweetly scented the local economy —literally. A former local bank employee recollected:

> You know most money is dirty. But Dell and her girls always wore perfume and the money they brought into the bank always made the place smell wonderful. The smell would last until the money had been withdrawn. It was always a rush in the morning to open up the vault and get the first whiff of perfume.

Despite her success, no one recalls Dell ever breaching the self-imposed bounds of propriety that made her as tough on employees as she was on herself. If, for example, one of her girls became intoxicated or obnoxious in a local bar, the young woman would be gone the next day. In response to a local curfew, she shut down her business promptly at midnight every night. And out of respect for churchgoers, she kept the hotel closed each Sunday. "That's so none of the boys come here instead of going to church," Dell once said. "I certainly wouldn't want any of my girls competing." Outside the hotel, her protegees always followed the boss's example by speaking only when spoken to first. With a touch of wistfulness, Dell once said of folks in town that "all they do is nod and smile." She also did not want any of her staff infected by venereal disease, nor did she want them to harm the customers. As a precaution, Dell hired local physicians such as Dr. Walter E. Reckling to regularly inspect and treat those who worked for her. Reflecting the current mores, the long-time Lusk physician later credited Dell's operation with curbing sex-related abuse and crimes that might otherwise have affected more respectable ladies and their daughters. The mother of Lusk resident Ed Ryder agreed. She supported Dell because, according to Ryder's son, the men "knew where they could go, and the women and young girls were safe to walk the streets." Another inviolate rule: to the best of anyone's knowledge, neither she or her girls ever divulged a customer's name, although Dell did single out an eighty-year-old out-of-towner as one of her best patrons.

Although Dell was a strict manager, her workers also remember how she cared for them. Dell regularly took her well-groomed girls to the XL Café for afternoon coffee, frequently using such get-togethers to give them informal lessons in table manners. She also took them on trips to her 415-acre ranch about three miles east of Lusk. There they lounged on the flagstone patio in the shade of birch and pine trees and, as the sun set, they ate steaks that Dell grilled on the barbecue. The women recalled such kindnesses in letters found in Dell's home following her death. "Apparently she was always giving them money, helping them when they were sick and urging them on to a better life," explained Helen Brummell, the estate sale clerk. "I also found boxes of toys that she had kept for her girls' kids," she added.

An air of care and concern veiled the almost painfully private and guarded woman whom few knew well. Those who made the effort to know Dell, however, reaped rewards. Others were struck by her sense of style; one columnist wrote, "Her hair was done up... not fanciful but well, and her face was unwrinkled. She dressed stylishly, but not gaudy." According to her hairdresser, Dell tried to arrive for appointments either early or late in the business day. Following each such visit, she took pains to inquire if any other customers had been offended by her presence. Although always subtly coiffed and modestly clad, Dell loved nice clothes, furs, and fine gems. Her closet and jewelry box attested to that fact. In the mid-1970s, a west coast writer who interviewed Dell found her paradoxically prudish in some ways. "Everything is sex now," she muttered with disgust. "You see much more on TV and in the movies than you see in my place. I don't care for it that way. Sex should be a private matter, not a public affair. Something behind closed doors, not in the open," she sniffed.

The shell of the infamous Yellow Hotel, which dated from the Lance Creek Oil Field boom days, still stands at 219 Griffith Boulevard in Lusk. In its glory days it attracted politicians, cattle barons, national guardsmen, and oil-patch workers alike. (Wyoming State Archives)

That sense of responsibility also set her apart from her peers in her profession. She strongly believed in sharing one's earnings with one's community. Frugal to the point of saving old newspapers, shopping bags, and assorted clutter, she nevertheless gave money anonymously and generously to poor families, churches, and nearly every local civic project. Dell also took under her wing two young men who eventually earned doctorates at Stanford and UCLA. Each Christmas they sent her cards and thanked her for funding their educations. Rumors persist she may have funded other scholars, too. And on New Year's Eve, without fanfare, she arranged for a corsage to be given to each woman who visited local bars. She even helped pay for a stone memorial for another Niobrara County madam, Mother Featherlegs.

On at least one occasion, Dell let compassion slip beyond mere charitable concern. Bronson "Jerry" Dull, an unlucky local oilfield worker, lost his right leg in an accident while off-loading a truck in

1930. Dell helped set Jerry up as a partner in the Oasis Bar and
Club, the billiard hall in Lusk's Ranger Hotel. They remained com-
panions and, according to Dell, planned to wed.

But Dull died of a heart attack on June 4, 1955, shortly before
the planned nuptials.

Thanks to her business acumen and the popularity of her Yellow
Hotel, Dell continued to prosper while many around her succumbed to the stock market crash of 1929, the subsequent ravages
of the Great Depression, and the lean years of World War II. "Mrs.
Burke," as folks increasingly called her, became a member in absen-
tia of the Lusk Chamber of Commerce and the Wyoming Farm
Bureau. She also joined the local country club, although no one
knew her to play golf.

As the banner days of Wyoming's oil boom waned in the late
1940s, Lusk's population slipped to fewer than sixteen hundred.
The dwindling economy and the lack of free-spending men had a
decidedly adverse affect on Dell's business. She swapped the dance
band for a jukebox and served her customers snacks instead of
gourmet meals. Her bevy of beauties also dwindled by the late
1970s to one or two women who, like circuit riders, came to service
the occasional paying customer during hunting season and annual
National Guard encampments. The mahogany-paneled main room
of the Yellow Hotel, its walls lined with reproductions of paintings
by Charles Russell and other western artists, rarely saw more than
one customer at a time.

However, having comfortably feathered her nest by investing
smartly in real estate, oil, and blue-chip stocks, Dell seemed to enjoy
her late-life leisure. And she had earned it, having managed one of
the most celebrated brothels in the state for nearly sixty years. She
spent more of her time traveling and entertaining friends or an occasional relative at her ranch. In retrospect, it seems that she had
finally found a home as happy as that of her youth in North
Dakota. Dell had but one regret: she never had a child.

On August 4, 1979, the aging, once-lusty lady tripped and fell
on the sidewalk in front of her hotel and broke a hip. Following

Dell (left) and Phyllis, her sister-in-law, visit the Texas Trail Monument just east of Lusk near Dell's small ranch. (Loraine A. Fisher collection.)

treatment at a Scottsbluff, Nebraska, hospital, she returned two weeks later to Lusk, where Dr. Kenneth Turner cared for her at Niobrara County Memorial Hospital. Once her health stabilized, she moved into the nursing home wing where the staff described her as a model patient, warmly accepted and highly respected. But Dell had not lost her snap, and those who forgot that fact frequently felt her sting. She told one well-intentioned matron who stopped by to read the Bible to her that she should "Get the hell out of my room …and turn on the TV as you leave!"

Despite the occasional flash of irascibility, Dell claimed in her clover years, "I wouldn't trade my life for anything. I'm glad of it. I've made a lot of money. Traveled the world. For me it's been a good life." Good, indeed! The executor of her estate valued it at nearly $1.3 million, which marked Dell one of the wealthiest self-made women in Wyoming.

But it all came to an end when the venerable madam succumbed at age ninety-three in her hospital room on Election Day,

The monument to "Mother Featherlegs" was paid for in part by Dell Burke who kept a low profile and chose not to attend its dedication on May 16, 1965. Later, with some of her lady employees and friends, Dell visited the marker, which can be found by traveling about two miles west of Lusk on U.S. Highway 20, then ten miles south on a dirt road. (Loraine A. Fisher Collection)

November 4, 1980. No one held a memorial service. No one sent flowers. Her family simply cremated her body and strew her ashes in the winds that blew across her beloved ranch land.

Shortly after the sale of Dell's personal possessions and properties in 1981, a group of good-humored Cheyenne ladies initiated an informal social group that they call the "Dell Burke Memorial Auxiliary." In honor of her spirit and *joie de vivre*, they periodically meet as a group to take lunch and shop. But perhaps the Auxiliary ladies' most celebrated get-together is their Frontier Days Buck-off which they created to honor Dell's memory each year as part of Cheyenne's famous rodeo.

❧ SOURCES CITED ❧ I have talked by phone with Loraine A. Fisher of Harrison, Michigan, about her great-aunt Marie Fisher Law, aka Dell Burke, on numerous occasions. She also shared with me Dell's family photo album and much family correspondence. Among the roughly

125 interviews I had with Dell's acquaintances, the most important were those with Margaret Lee of Torrington, Wyoming, on November 5, 1993; Charles Hillinger of Rancho Palos Verdes, California, on December 13, 1993; former Niobrara County Sheriff Harold E. Rogers on December 30, 1993; Thelma Jean Bales of Laramie on January 12, 1994; James Fagan of Casper on January 14, 1994; Bob Darrow of Denver on January 19, 1994; Wyoming Supreme Court Justices William A. Taylor and William H. Smith of Cheyenne, both on January 24, 1994; Mildred Ladwig of Lance Creek, Wyoming, on January 25, 1994; and Helen E. Brummell of Torrington, Wyoming, on January 26, 1994. I also talked to one of her former accountants, Bruce Bergstrom of Greybull, Wyoming, on January 16, 1994; he subsequently gave me a copy of the tape-recorded recollections he made shortly after one of his last meetings with his client.

I also studied numerous documents that recorded landmarks in Dell's life, items such as her Application for a Marriage License and her Certificate of Marriage, Walsh County Court, Grafton, North Dakota, dated November 11 and November 12, 1905, respectively; the Niobrara County District Court Case Files #50-112 and #C-1232; Council Proceedings, City of Lusk, Vol. 3, June 14, 1929; Certificate of Death, Mary Fisher Law aka Del [sic] Burke, Niobrara County Probate Docket #3-164, Lusk; and Last Will and Testament of Dell Burke, December 20, 1979, Niobrara County Probate Docket #3-1674, Lusk.

Many articles shed light on Dell's life, colorful personality, and the company she kept. These include "Jerry Dull Badly Hurt in Accident at Casper July 24," *Lusk Free Lance*, July 31, 1930; Charles Hillinger's "A Sporting House Madam for 54 Years," and "Everybody Likes Dell—but Most Avoid Her," *Los Angeles Times*, March 26, 1973; "Obituaries: Del [sic] Burke," *Lusk Herald*, November 13, 1980; Red Fenwick's "Dell's Profession No Embarrassment…the Madam Was a Well-heeled Lady," *Denver Post*, December 21, 1980; Red Fenwick's "Buyers to Blitz Bordello Booty," *Denver Post*, August 2, 1981; Mark Bagne, "Red Light Days Are Recalled at Auction," *Wyoming Tribune-Eagle*, Cheyenne, August 16, 1981; "Wyoming Town Finds Bonanza

Dell loved to travel and made treks to many parts of the world. Here, she relaxes in Acapulco, Mexico. (Loraine A. Fisher collection)

in Bordello," *New York Times*, August 16, 1981; Ron Franscell's "Last Bawdy House Trinkets Gone, But Memories Linger," *Casper Star-Tribune*, August 17, 1981; and "Dell Burke Estate Auction Is Featured in 'Stars and Stripes,'" *Lusk Herald*, September 3, 1981.

Walter Jones's *The Sandbar* (Casper, WY: Baso, Inc., 1981); Douglas A. Wick's *North Dakota Place Names* (Bismarck, ND: Hede Markan Collectibles, 1988); and Sue F. Ellis's "Dell Burke's Yellow Hotel," (unpublished manuscript, Stagecoach Museum, Lusk, WY, January 5, 1989), proved much background about her "professional" life as well as that of many of her associates.

This chapter first appeared, in a slightly different form, in *Wyoming Annals* (Vol. 66, No. 4), Winter 1994-1995.

L ARRY K. BROWN, author of six books, has also written nonfiction articles for such periodicals as *Wild West, True West, Old West, American Cowboy, Cowboy,* the National Cowboy Hall of Fame's *Persimmon Hill, Roundup* of Western Writers of America, *Wyoming Magazine, Annals of Wyoming, Wyoming History Journal, Compton's Encyclopedia Yearbook,* the *NOLA Quarterly,* and *WOLA Journal.* His short stories have been published in the prestigious *High Plains Register* literary-arts magazine.

Brown's book *Hog Ranches of Wyoming: Liquor, Lust, and Lies Under Sagebrush Skies* (High Plains Press, 1995) was honored with the Western Horizon Award from Wyoming Writers, Inc. Cambridge University Press in England, the oldest press in the world, selected the book's text for inclusion in its computerized lexicon, a database used by language researchers in creating dictionaries and other reference books for students of English as a second language.

High Plains Press also published Brown's *You Are Respectfully Invited to Attend My Execution* (1997) and *Petticoat Prisoners of Old Wyoming* (2001). The latter, which received the 2001 Wyoming State Historical Society's Publications Award, was based on Brown's *Petticoat Prisoners of the Wyoming Frontier Prison.* Both books tell the stories of inmates in the Wyoming's dreaded Territorial and State Penitentiaries. And Brown recently finished a book of short stories that deal with the revenge of those who turned up their toes in *Sagebrush Seasons.*

Brown served as membership chairman for Western Writers of America. He and his wife, Florence, make their home in Cheyenne. They have four grown children.

MICHAEL J. SULLIVAN ("Mike") is a third-generation Wyoming-ite born in 1939 to a legal family with deep roots in the state. His grandfather was a lawyer in Laramie and his father practiced law in Douglas where Mike grew up. He earned a B.S. in Petroleum Engineering (1961) and his J.D. with honors (1964) from the University of Wyoming. He practiced at the Casper firm of Brown, Drew, Apostolos, Massey & Sullivan (1964–1986) and was elected to two terms as Wyoming's governor (1987–1995). His reelection was by the largest margin in the state's history.

He was a fellow of the Institute of Politics at Harvard's Kennedy School of Government (1996) and served as U. S. Ambassador to Ireland (1999–2001), returning to Casper in September 2001, where he joined the regional law firm of Rothgerber Johnson & Lyons as special counsel.

He is a passionate fly-fisherman, hunter, and golfer. He and his wife Jane have three grown children, Michelle, Patrick, and Theresa, and four grandchildren.

❧ NOTES ON THE PRODUCTION OF THIS BOOK ❧

Coyotes & Canaries was simultaneously released in two editions.

A *limited edition* of 200 copies of this volume was Smythe sewn,
bound in Gingerbread Kivar 7 with a Grand Levant texture,
and embossed with copper foil.
Each copy is signed by the author and hand numbered.
This limited edition was issued with no dust jacket.

The *softcover trade edition* is covered with ten-point stock,
printed in four colors, and finished with a lay-flat gloss coating.

The text of both editions is composed with
twelve-point type from the Garamond Family by Adobe.
Display type is Curlz by Monotype and Adobe Trajan
with ornaments from Poetica by Adobe.